The Secret to Healthy Relationships

The Secret to Healthy Relationships

Margaret Mendenhall

YorkshirePublishing
www.yorkshirepublishing.com
Write Now

Yorkshire Publishing
3207 South Norwood Avenue
Tulsa, Oklahoma 74135
www.YorkshirePublishing.com
918.394.2665

Dedicated to my husband, Charlie, who started me
on this wonderful adventure in relationships and has
weathered the storms with me for the past fifty-five years.

Acknowledgments

Thank you, Charlie, for releasing me from my household responsibilities so I could have the quiet time I needed to write this book. For all the times you had to fry your own egg, make your own salad, and feed my cats so I could be gone, you are greatly appreciated.

Thanks to Linda Shoulders, who took a manuscript written by a grandmother who studied grammar over sixty years ago and opened up a whole new concept of commas and semicolons.

Thank you, Kim, for lending your time and talent to help put the finishing touches on this book. I desperately needed your expert advice and experience.

Thanks to our three amazing children, Quentin, Brad, and Kim, who taught me that growing in relationships can be fun, who proved that in a world of strife and division, they had sense enough to choose outstanding spouses.

Thanks to our two daughters-in-law, Trisha and Tamy, and son-in-law, Eugene, who have demonstrated what relationships in marriage were meant to be.

Thanks to our sixteen incredible grandchildren: Joshua and wife Dainele, Keelie and husband Seth, Brooke and husband Kinsley, Brittany and husband Lenny, Brandon, Bryce, CE, Zack and wife Lynette, Ezekiel, Justin, and Matthew, who have made learning how to function in relationships worthwhile. You are our pride and joy and have defined the genuine meaning of love. It has been a delight to watch you grow in the Lord and become stable and secure young men and women who are now experiencing successful relationships of your own.

And to our remarkable great-granddaughters, Hadley Grace and Iba Jade and great-grandson, Kaden King, who in the early stages of their lives, are surrounded with family who love them dearly and model relationships based on the God kind of love, you are blessed beyond measure.

Thanks to all the wonderful people at Victory Center who walked with me through this exciting adventure, encouraging and praying for me while I completed this project—especially my faithful prayer partners Mary Lou, Ellen, and Sharon.

Finally, I am eternally grateful to the Holy Spirit whose hand I felt on my shoulder many times when the writing became difficult and the words got entangled in the shadowy corners of my mind and refused to emerge. You inspired me, anointed me, and never let me down.

Contents

1

Broken Dreams

"God, am I losing my mind?" I stared with unseeing eyes out my kitchen window while tears spilled down my cheeks, making tiny ripples in the dirty dishwater. *"Why do I feel like I'm falling apart?"* I wiped the tears on my sleeve. Outside, the sun kissed the emerald leaves of the gnarled elm tree gracing our modest ranch house; but inside, at least in my heart, the mood was anything but sunny.

The cry of my heart was sincere that day as my disillusioned mind viewed a heap of crumpled dreams piled at my feet. As a young girl, I had visualized the day when I would have my own home, complete with a doting husband who pampered and loved me, adorable children who cooed and gurgled with pleasure every time they sensed my devoted presence—but then, I got married and woke up. Reality painted a much bleaker picture than the fantasies that had floated through my childish mind.

I was nineteen years old when Charlie and I married. Right away, I got the feeling my "live happily ever after" storybook fantasy was not happening the way I had written it in my head. My husband was a cowboy—I'm talking old-fashioned, get-dirty, cow-manure-polluted, boot-wearing, horse-loving cowboy. He was a wonderful man, but romance for him was a potted plant and an occasional "this sure is good cookin'" compliment offered when he especially enjoyed a home-cooked meal.

That was not what I had in mind. Romance for me was a candlelight dinner, complete with roses, sitting enraptured while gazing into each other's eyes, with sparks flying, goose bumps popping, angels singing, and moonlight glowing—all the wonderful things I read about in the romantic novels I had devoured as a teenager. Was I ever disillusioned. Sometimes, my husband even committed the unpardonable sin by forgetting to buy me a valentine's card on February the fourteenth. And heaven help him if he neglected to get me a birthday card on my special day.

Then the kids started coming. The part about them being adorable was accurate, but the cooing and gurgling? Well, that only happened when they were well-fed, diapers dry and free of all offensive debris, and conditions conducive to a split second of maternal bonding amid dirty dishes, smelly clothes, and surroundings cluttered with diaper pail, lotions, baby oil, and tubes of Desitin ointment.

My coping mechanism was severely impaired. I honestly thought I was losing my mind. At times, while riding down the highway, I could feel my consciousness escape for just a second into a place where only silence reigned and feelings numb—but only for an instant, and then everything would be back to normal. For me, normal was feeling out of control, overwhelmed, and confused, with a low-level gnawing fear, believing I had to do everything right, but not quite able to pull it off.

Finally, amid frustration and disappointment, I came to the conclusion that the only way out of my dilemma was to take the kids and run away from home—like I could leave all my problems behind if I went somewhere else.

But God had other plans. He didn't look at me as a hopeless case destined to search frantically for illusive happiness in relationship after relationship only to become more and more broken with each successive failure. He had a wonderful plan to take a self-disillusioned misfit and give her an extreme makeover. The procedure started in 1973 on Easter Sunday night.

In the bedroom of our ranch house, twenty miles south of Perryton, Texas, I had an encounter with Jesus. I had been agonizing in prayer for several weeks. I didn't know just what I needed, but I knew I had to have something. Easter night of that year, while lying in bed in my shorty nightgown beside my sleeping husband, I prayed a silent prayer that changed my life: *Lord, I want the closest experience I can have with you.*

I had hardly finished my whispered prayer when a light filled the room. There in the midst of the light, I became aware of the presence of Jesus. That night, I was gloriously baptized by the Holy Spirit, not just sprinkled or daubed, but immersed and saturated in the Pentecostal way, like in the Acts 2:4 upper room. That experience blew my denominational theology to smithereens. But as a result, I found out something important—Jesus knew my name, where I lived, and he cared about me. I had given my life to Jesus when I was eight years old and was born again at that time. But as a result of the glorious experience I had on that Easter night, I fell in love with the Savior I had known so little about all those years.

Then my journey began in earnest. The most drastic change impacting my life, my marriage and consequently every other relationship, was when the Holy Spirit downloaded God's plan for relationships. That's what this book is about.

Recently, when a young lady in the medical profession learned I was writing a book about relationships, she asked if I was a psychologist. For just a moment, I had a twinge of misgiving concerning my credentials when I realized she must think only those in that particular field were qualified to address relationship problems. After all, I didn't have a PhD, MA, Dr., or any other impressive title before or after my name. I was simply an ordinary person who had walked through the valleys of pain, offense, betrayal, misunderstanding, frustration, tribulation, trials, and distress, and made it through unharmed, thanks to the grace of God.

As a result, I had a firm, unshakable assurance that God's way is the only way that brings peace and harmony in any relationship. The closest thing I have to a title in front of my name is Reverend, and that only represents a mandate from God to share the truths he teaches me with anyone who will listen.

The information written in this book was not learned while lying on a psychiatrist's couch, nor did I get it by sitting across the desk of a marriage counselor. Even though both of those sources have merit, my information was wrestled out piece by piece every time I had a head-on collision with barricades of negative behavior patterns. I stumbled and fell. I screamed out in agony more times than I would like to admit. Bloodied and battered emotionally and spiritually, amid tears of frustration and pain, I sent up heartrending prayers again and again to the only one who could help. And God never let me down. Oh yes, he most generally reprimanded and corrected me, but in the long run, he gave me the valuable information I so desperately needed.

Along the way, he also furnished the grace to implement it. Thus, my relationships started to change because I changed!

Incidentally, my cowboy-turned-preacher husband developed into a practicing romantic. Roses have replaced potted plants. Though the candlelight dinners are few and far between, there are still some noticeable sparks and occasionally, some interesting goose bumps.

Relationships were designed by God to be good, but sin made them dysfunctional. Thus, we have a world filled with hurt and misery. Choosing to crucify the flesh in our life that screams for gratification might not seem the most appealing way off the merry-go-round of pain and disappointment, but the path of peace is well worth it.

This book is designed to empower you to enjoy the blessings healthy relationships provide and help you escape the strongholds of any wrong thinking that keep you on the torture wheel of destructive behavior. When that happens, you might not have a PhD after your name either, but you will have succeeded in obtaining a remarkable achievement—you're an overcomer!

2

The Law

Someone once said, "God and I have a wonderful relationship. It's people who mess it up." In a world filled with imperfect, immature, and inconsistent inhabitants, it's no wonder that it takes only two individuals to twist a relationship into something that can be more painful than a toothache and more annoying than a cricket chirping at midnight. Many times, on the surface, a couple may look as if all the wrinkles have been smoothly pressed and ironed out, but in truth, serious problems may be stuffed beneath the surface, camouflaged with an isn't-life-wonderful disguise.

Todd and Debbie were like that. When they started attending our church, we thought they were the ideal couple. Outwardly, it appeared they had everything going for them.

They were a handsome pair with great personalities who had outstanding potential in every area. Todd worked at a lucrative job; and Debbie, who was exceptionally talented, supplemented their income in a business she started on her own. Looking on, one would say they were living a storybook life. However, all was not as it seemed. One day, Todd showed up at our door in tears. He sorrowfully announced that Debbie had left him and the kids, and was filing for divorce. His countenance showed deep hurt as he confessed his inability to grasp what had gone wrong. We listened, talked, and prayed with him, and after a while, I agreed to meet with Debbie.

A few days later, when I sat across from her, I looked into the eyes of someone else wounded and disillusioned with obvious signs of growing bitterness. As Debbie opened up to me, she told how her husband had hurled innuendos, put-downs, and sarcasm at her for years. He had either been indifferent to her pain or simply insensitive to her needs. She had put up with that form of abuse for quite a while and probably meted out some of her own as she endeavored to alleviate the hurt and disappointment of a relationship gone sour. The marriage was over as far as she was concerned. I could see she was not ready to hear or receive advice or take even one step toward salvaging their tattered relationship. I prayed with her and let her go hoping that at some future date, they would come to their senses and make the changes necessary to rebuild what the devil and ignorance had destroyed.

You will notice I mentioned *ignorance,* along with the devil, as being the culprit behind the demolition of relationships. If a couple doesn't know what it takes to build and nurture a healthy relationship, that *lack of knowledge* becomes an open invitation to the destroyer, giving him the opportunity to wreak havoc in the lives and homes of even Christians.

Debbie and Todd were Christians. Going to church had been part of their normal routine. However, they had drifted away from the Lord to some degree before their breakup. They were like most people who entered marriage with good intentions. Their desire was to be fulfilled and happy, but didn't have a clue how to sustain or nurture the relationship. That ignorance kept them from taking advantage of the many benefits God had in mind when he created the first couple.

God was the one who thought up relationships. In the beginning, he moved through the first five days of creation seamlessly. On the sixth day, with a grand flourish, he created man. After observing the crown of his creation, he stopped. Until then, he had pronounced "it is good" about everything he created. But with the creation of man, he saw something important was missing. Then God proclaimed, "It is not good for man to be alone; I will make him a help meet" (see Gen. 2:18).

After God administrated divine anesthetic, he reached into Adam's side and extracted a rib. With it, he fashioned a woman. When God presented Eve to her husband, Adam managed to mumble something about that gorgeous creature being bone of his bone and flesh of his flesh. Thus, the first human relationship was born.

However, today it's obvious that relationships are in trouble. The National Center for Health Statistics released a report in 2015 which found that roughly 40 percent of first marriages ended in separation or divorce within the first fifteen years. Besides that, there are numerous disillusioned and embittered children who are abused and run away from home every year. We are horrified at the accounts of random school shootings and almost every day, witness news reports of gruesome murders that flash across our television screens. With such widespread conflict happening regularly we would have to be blind not to realize relationships are being ripped apart at the seams while a world that doesn't have a clue struggles to find an answer.

You might think something as important as relationships would come with some kind of booklet complete with warnings and instructions. When I buy something as insignificant as a curling iron or a toaster, inserted in the packing is a little pamphlet complete with cautions and directions explaining how to operate the appliance for maximum efficiency. We need something like that for relationships.

Thankfully, God is practical. He would never create anything as significant as a relationship without a manual. It's not just a skimpy little pamphlet either. It's a complete what-to-do and what-not-to-do instruction book with rules and laws that, when followed correctly, create an atmosphere for relationships to work flawlessly, just the way God intended. That handbook is the Bible.

The whole Bible is a book about relationships. First, it's about our relationship with God, and secondly, it gives specific instructions concerning our association with other people. The most significant law pertaining to human relationships is written in Galatians 5:14. "For the whole Law (concerning human relationships) is complied with in the one precept, you shall love your neighbor as (you do) yourself."

That's the law. A law of God is not just a splendid suggestion. Any law that originates with God is irrefutable. You might not like it or even understand it, but if you break it, there are consequences.

The law of gravity is another one of those undeniable laws. You might be on the tenth floor of a high-rise building and decide you don't want to take the elevator to the ground floor, instead you elect to take a shortcut and walk off the balcony. You may be ignorant of the law of gravity or a little fed up with all its demands; but whether you like it or not, if you break it, you are going to get hurt.

The law governing relationships operates the same way. You might not like the restrictions it puts on your behavior, but if you don't follow the rules, it's certain you will get hurt.

In life, there are many opportunities to get injured, and numerous occasions arise where you can hurt others as well. With the many people we have to deal with, it's no wonder we're presented with so many challenges. It's like the nerve-wracking experience of driving on a busy winding mountain highway. As harrowing as it might be meeting a steady stream of traffic, you usually arrive at your destination safe and intact with very little effort. Every car or truck you meet has the potential to cause serious damage if it should wander into your lane; however, as long as you both stay in your respective lanes, you can pass without incident. But if either of you trespass into the other's lane, there will be a head-on collision, unless one of you hits the ditch.

Walking in love is a two-lane road where relationships are concerned. Both individuals have a side. When one person selfishly demands the whole highway, that relationship is in danger of being wrecked, unless the other party makes allowances and hits the ditch by forgiving.

In order to build healthy relationships, it is in our best interest to learn all we can about the crucial law that governs relationships. When we turn sixteen and think we are grown-up enough to drive a car, we're required by law to take a driver's test. We have to study the rules of the highway and learn everything we can about them. Finally, we must pass a written and driving test before we are issued a license.

The world would be better off if we were required to study the laws regarding human relationships before we are given a license to love. That's not the case, however.

We are thrown into a world teeming with countless other characters just as ignorant as we are. With that much lack of knowledge, how can we expect to escape wreckage from the inevitable collisions we will experience in our lifetime?

In Matthew 22, a lawyer approached Jesus asking him which commandment was the greatest. Jesus answered in verses 37–40:

> You shall love the Lord your God with all your heart and with all your soul and with all your mind (intellect). This is the great (most important, principal) and first commandment. And a second is like it: You shall love your neighbor as [you do] yourself. These two commandments sum up and upon them depend all the Law and the Prophets.

When God gives us an enormous task, such as getting along with others, he makes it simple. Just one precept with two parts: love God and love people. Sounds pretty simple, but *it is easier read than done!*

Jesus Loves Me This I Know

Success in keeping that commandment pivots on one foundational truth: the love of God. First, you must know that God loves you with a love not based on your performance or your station in life. It's important you come to the realization that God loves you just the way you are, unconditionally, with no strings attached.

You can be certain God's love is not based on how good you are by reading what the Bible records in Romans 5:8: "But God shows and clearly proves His (own) love for us by the fact that while we were still sinners Christ, the Messiah, the Anointed One, died for us."

Even while we were sinners and could do nothing right, God loved us so much he sacrificed his only son for us.

If he loved us that much *before* we were his children why would he withdraw his love when we did something wrong *after* we were his children? God's love is unconditional. It's not based on our behavior or character but based on God's nature. In 1 John 4:8, it states, "God is love." That's what he is, and that's what he does.

When you grasp the fact that God genuinely loves you, it becomes easier to obey the first part of that important law enabling you to love God fervently. It's only natural to love someone who loves you. That's why the apostle John said in 1 John 4:19, "We love Him, because He first loved us."

In order to apply the law of relationships properly, it can't be done with the flawed and unstable human love we are most familiar with. It takes a more complete love than that—*perfect* love to be exact. Perfect love is quite rare in our world. It's a commodity that can't be worked up, manufactured by human efforts, or even willed to be. That kind of love comes from God. In 1 John 4:7, it reads, "Beloved, let us love one another, for love is (springs) from God."

Drawing from the Well of Love

When God created mankind, a vibrant love connection existed between God and man. Adam and Eve's need for love was adequately filled every day when God visited them for a time of fellowship in the cool of the evening. Since God is love and the only source of complete, perfect love comes from a close relationship with him, their love cup was always filled to the brim. When sin entered the garden severing man's heart connection with God, it cut off Adam and Eve's source of love. They were left with a huge need and only frail humans to fill it.

To attempt to get your love void filled from another human being is fruitless and disappointing. Human love always fails at some point. The Lord spoke to me about this subject:

"There is no other source of true agape, unselfish love, except that which comes from me. Anytime you experience that kind of love from a human, you can know they have allowed my love to flow out of them—but I am still the source. Any other kind of love, apart from my love, is only a selfish, grasping love that is a poor substitute for real love and will never bring satisfaction.

"More people would be able to allow my love to flow from them into the lives of others if their hearts were not so clogged with selfishness. That's why it is rare to find anyone who has a complete flow of love pouring from the rivers of their heart. Because of this, it is futile to depend on human love to satisfy your thirst for love. It seldom happens.

"The best way to get satisfaction is to go straight to the never-ending supply, a river that has an abundant measure with no blockages of any kind. You need a source you can depend on that will never fail. That bottomless well is the love flowing from my heart to yours. It will meet any need you have for love.

"My love will fill you to the full. Instead of being an empty reservoir, you will become a channel that can readily overflow into the lives of others who are thirsty, empty, and dry. My love in you will be someone else's source of supply. When you do this, my child, I can assure you, you will never run dry!"

Understanding the Characteristics of God's kind of Love

Our inability to develop and release the love of God often comes from a faulty understanding of its characteristics.

When my husband and I first became pastors, many who came to me for counseling about relationship problems had obvious attitudes of bitterness and resentment. But they would often say, "I just walked in love."

On the inside, I thought, *you call that love. I don't think so.*

Then there were times when I thought I was doing a great job of demonstrating love, but my husband said, "Well, it would help if you would just walk in love!"

I thought, *Hey! I am walking in love. I'm gritting my teeth, biting my tongue, and not saying what I'd like to say.*

That's when I realized, we in the body of Christ don't know much about how the real God kind of love acts. While pondering this, I heard the Spirit of God whisper, "It would help if you knew what the *opposite* of love is."

I thought I knew the answer to that one. I had supposed *hate* was the opposite of love, and I didn't hate anyone. So did that mean I always walked in love?

Then I remembered that God's love was on display in its greatest and highest form in John 3:16: "For God so loved the world that He gave his only begotten Son, that whosoever believeth in Him should not perish, but have everlasting life" (kjv).

I had hardly finished quoting that familiar scripture when I saw it: God so loved that he *gave.* God's love is a "giving, self-sacrificing" love, so the opposite would have to be "taking" or "self-centered." Then I had it: the opposite of the God kind of love wasn't hate after all; it was *selfishness.*

After that revelation, I needed to see a clear description of how selfishness behaves. First Corinthians 13:4–8 paints a well-defined portrait of God's love, and since selfishness is the opposite of agape love, I decided to take each word describing love and find the opposite meaning to get a picture of selfishness. What took shape was surprisingly accurate in spelling out the ugly characteristics of selfishness. This is what emerged:

A person who is selfish...

...is irritable and grouchy, impatient and unkind (has bad moods);

...is envious and possessive, jealous and indifferent to the needs of others;

...is withdrawn and arrogant, exalts self, thinks he is better than others;

...has to always be right and is defensive when challenged;

...is rude and flares up easily;

...always insists on his own rights and his own way;

...thinks only of his own needs or wants, and demands they be met;

...is easily upset or hurt;

...frets when circumstances are not going right;

...allows resentment to remain in his heart;

keeps count of suffered wrongs and nourishes them;

...takes secret satisfaction when misfortune comes to the disobedient (says, "It serves them right!");

...is skeptical when right and truth prevails (says, "It won't last!");

...can't cope with life's ups and downs;

...believes every bad thing he hears about others;

...assigns the worst motives to others instead of believing the best;

...majors on the faults of others;

...acts and reacts as circumstances dictates

Selfishness never wins; it always fails!

Selfishness is a problem common to mankind. When Adam and Eve allowed sin to come into their lives, they no longer focused on their relationship with God; instead, they hid from him. Disobedience caused our first parents to lose their God-consciousness and become self-conscious. As a result, every baby born from their seed thereafter had his or her nature contaminated with the relationship-destroying cancer of selfishness. This became evident right away in Adam and Eve's first two children; one wound up killing the other. Relationship problems had begun even back then.

Remedy for Selfishness

Since mankind is infected with the plague of selfishness, how do we get rid of it? There is a simple remedy: selfishness must be displaced with the God kind of love. In any given situation, we either walk in love or operate out of selfishness; both can't function in a person's life at the same time.

We read in Romans 5:5, "God's love has been poured out in our hearts by the Holy Spirit Who has been given to us."

When a person is born again, God restores the most vital attribute lost to the human race as the result of Adam and Eve's sin. When you made Jesus Christ your Lord, you were given a new nature by the Holy Spirit. Embedded in the heart of every believer is a reservoir of God's love. However, a Christian can go a lifetime never using it and continue to be as selfish as before.

It's like having your house plumbed with running water. There's an abundant supply of water readily available any time you want it, but you will never enjoy it until you turn on the faucet. If you're a child of God, you have been plumbed with the love of God, but you have a choice whether or not to turn on the faucet and allow it to flow. John addresses this in 1 John 3:17–18:

> But if anyone has this world's goods—resources for sustaining life—and sees his brother and fellow believer in need, yet closes his heart of compassion against him, how can the love of God live and remain in him? Little children, let us not love (merely) in theory or in speech but in deed and in truth—in practice and in sincerity.

To lay an immovable foundation upon which to build strong, healthy relationships, the habit of living in the love of God and letting it flow out to others is essential. That's the law, and that's the only way to cultivate and nurture something that will last. Paul writes in 1 Corinthians 13:8, "Love never fails—never fades out or becomes obsolete or comes to an end." If a relationship is built on love (God's kind of love) then it is built on something that will never fail, diminish, or come to an end.

In the case of Todd and Debbie, after a few years of misery and confusion, they remarried. They finally got it right. Today, they are happily married and on fire for God, serving him in a local church. Todd and Debbie are examples of a couple who found it is never too late to implement the law of human relationships in marriage. They know firsthand, when you break that irrefutable law, you get hurt. But now that they have learned how to put into practice that law in their marriage, they are enjoying the huge dividends it produces.

Love Works by Faith

It takes a measure of faith to appropriate anything God makes available. The best way to release faith in the area of walking in love is to pray the prayer that Paul prayed for the Philippians. This prayer has brought about tremendous results, not only in me but for others when I pray it over them.

Prayer to develop God's love in your life from Philippians 1:9–11 (AMP):

> Father, I pray that your love will be developed more and more in my life and come to full outward manifestation, so I can learn to sense what is vital and approve and prize what is excellent and of real value, recognizing the highest and the best, and distinguishing the moral differences, so I can approach the day of Jesus Christ not stumbling or causing others to stumble. I pray that I might abound and be filled with fruits of righteousness so Christ's glory may be both manifested and recognized in me.

What happens when you pray that prayer from you heart? If you sincerely want to get rid of selfishness and enjoy the benefits of living in God's love, get ready for the ride of your life. God will take your prayer seriously exposing you to various flesh-crucifying opportunities. That's the surgery part when selfishness is laid out on the operating table and you undergo the systematic disconnection of one uncaring tentacle at a time. In the process, an abundance of God's grace will be released into your soul enabling you to do what you couldn't do on your own. The results will be an incredible makeover.

I heard a story of a middle-aged woman who had a heart attack and was taken to the hospital. While on the operating table, she had a near-death experience. Seeing God, she asked, "Is my time up?" God said, "No, you have another forty-three years, two months and eight days to live." Upon recovery, the woman decided to stay in the hospital and have a face-lift, nose job, liposuction, breast enlargement, and a tummy tuck. Since she had so much more time to live, she figured she might as well look her best. After her last operation, she was released from the hospital. While crossing the street on her way home, an ambulance hit and killed her. Arriving in front of God, she demanded, "I thought you said I had another forty plus years? Why didn't you pull me out of the path of that ambulance?" God replied, "I would have, but girl I didn't recognize you!"

That's a humorous account of the drastic difference a physical makeover can produce. However, the most beneficial change a person can experience is the inward one. That's the kind that changes attitudes, thought patterns, and the behavior of an individual, transforming them from a miserable, self-cherishing person into a loving, caring, and forgiving companion. That's extreme. An alteration of that type turns a shrew into a saint, a controller into a servant, and a sinner into the genuine likeness of Jesus.

You've learned about the law governing human relationships, what it is and what it isn't. Now you're ready to take that knowledge and use it to begin your own personal makeover by implementing it in the everyday struggles and challenges of life. Prepare to become skilled at wearing the love of God like a shield when the battles of life threaten to overwhelm you and how to use it offensively and defensively against anything and everything that is hurled against you by the enemy of your soul, including how to deal with those inconsiderate, obstinate people the devil uses to do his dirty work.

Comparison between Agape Love and Selfishness

"Love endures long and is patient and kind."
> Selfishness is irritable and cannot endure opposition.
> Selfishness is impatient with others to the point of being unkind.

"Love is never envious nor boils over with jealousy."
> Selfishness desires things that others have.
> Selfishness is possessive and is often filled with jealousy.

"Love is not boastful or vain glorious. Love does not display itself haughtily."
> Selfishness wants to talk only about itself and its interests, its accomplishments and is disdainful and cold.
> Selfishness is prideful and conducts itself in a high and distant manner.

"Love is not conceited, arrogant, or inflated with pride."
> Selfishness has an extremely high opinion of itself. It is overbearing and filled with pride.

"Love is not rude or unmannerly, and does not act unbecomingly."
> Selfishness will often appear rude and unmannerly, even to its family. Sometimes, selfishness acts unbecoming by throwing temper tantrums.

"Love [God's love in us] does not insist on its own rights. Love does not insist on its own way, for it is not self-seeking."

Selfishness insists on its own rights and its own way, with no regard for the feelings, opinions, or needs of others. It seeks only its own wants or desires.

"Love is not touchy, fretful, or resentful."

Selfishness is easily upset and hurt. It frets when things are not going right and allows resentment to lodge and build in its heart.

"Love takes no account of the evil done to it. Love pays no attention to a suffered wrong."

Selfishness counts up and takes note of evil done to it and nourishes a suffered wrong.

"Love does not rejoice at injustice and unrighteousness, but love rejoices when right and truth prevails."

Selfishness takes secret satisfaction when someone else gets his just due.

Selfishness does not rejoice but is skeptical when right and truth prevails.

"Love bears up under anything and everything that comes."

Selfishness is unstable and cannot cope with life's ups and downs.

"Love is ever ready to believe the best of every person."

Selfishness believes and relishes every tidbit of gossip about anyone and passes it on as truth.

Selfishness refuses to see the potential in people but majors on their faults.

"Love's hopes are fadeless under all circumstances."

Selfishness acts and reacts as circumstances dictate.

"Love endures everything without weakening."

Everything selfishness tries to produce fails.

Love never fails! Selfishness never wins!

3

Loving Yourself

One of our grandsons, Ezekiel, or Zeke as we call him, is intelligent, analytical and imaginative—and very different from his four brothers. Of the four temperaments: sanguine, choleric, melancholy and phlegmatic, his personality is predominantly melancholy. As a result, he tends to be creative and has a predisposition to consider it necessary to do everything just right. Because his love language is "words of affirmation," he needs those around him to approve of his behavior.

Obviously, he couldn't do everything right during his childhood, so he had to be corrected and reprimanded from time to time. His brothers took disciplinary action in stride as a normal part of life, but not Zeke. It devastated him. When he did anything wrong, he felt he had failed, not only his parents but God as well. He had a tendency to think of himself as a bad boy instead of a good person.

At six years of age, he developed severe problems with depression. He couldn't understand how God could forgive him for all the things he had done wrong, probably because he couldn't forgive himself for falling short of perfection. He knew he wanted to go to heaven, but in his heart, he couldn't believe he would ever be "good enough." His mother explained to him that no one was good enough to go to heaven, even the best people on earth couldn't make it to heaven unless they accepted the sacrifice Jesus provided for their sins. Zeke listened, but still, the wall in his young mind wouldn't come down. Convinced he was not a good boy, no amount of reasoning could persuade him otherwise. Many times at night, he burst out crying. When his parents asked him what was wrong, he answered, "I don't think you love me."

Even when his mother and father reassured him time and time again they loved him, reminding him that he could be forgiven for anything he had done, the depression continued night after night. We suspected he was listening to the lies of the devil and took authority over a deceiving spirit, but still, the episodes continued.

During the weeks of that family crisis, my daughter talked to me quite often. We searched for a solution to Zeke's problem, but nothing we tried or any prayers we prayed seemed to make a difference. The situation progressed until on one occasion he locked himself in the bathroom, declaring he was going to kill himself. We were alarmed. How could that be happening to our little grandson who lived in a vibrant Christian home, surrounded by a family who really did care deeply for him?

A few days later, while making preparations for our daughter and boys to come for a visit, I seriously interceded for Zeke. The situation had just come to a head with the threat of suicide, so my prayers were more urgent than usual. As I walked through the house praying, my attention was drawn to a bag stashed in the corner of the room.

Days before, while in a local gift shop, I had seen an adorable stuffed puppy with his head hanging out of a cardboard doghouse. For some reason, I felt compelled to purchase the dog with no idea what to do with it. That day, while praying, I heard the Holy Spirit whisper, "Give that puppy to Zeke." I argued for the space of a minute. I didn't know if he even liked stuffed animals. Besides, what did that have to do with anything?

Finally, I agreed to give the puppy to him. As soon as I decided to obey God, the Holy Spirit gave me a message for Zeke. The next day when they arrived, sure enough, Zeke was the very picture of depression. His head hung down. He shuffled when he walked, didn't smile, and wouldn't respond to my hugs.

When they got ready to leave, I motioned for Zeke to follow me into the bedroom. I told him God had directed me to buy the present I had in the bag for a very special boy. When I pulled the puppy from the sack, Zeke's eyes lit up and a big grin spread across his face. I asked, "Do you believe Mimi hears from God?" He nodded, so I read him the message from God:

"Tell Zeke I made him different from his brothers. I made him that way for a reason. He is not like any of his brothers because I made him for a special purpose. I put some unique gifts and talents inside that will set him apart and make him into the man I created him to be.

"The devil knows how valuable those qualities are, so he has worked hard to convince Ezekiel that he is worthless. As a result, Zeke doesn't like himself very much. He believes no one else likes him or loves him either, and that even I do not love him. Tell him none of that is true because he is very much loved. If he were standing next to Jesus, I would not love him any less than I love my son Jesus.

"He needs to know that this gift (the little stuffed puppy) is just one of many he will receive from me throughout his lifetime. If he will keep his eyes open, and not believe the devil's lies, I will bless him with many love gifts along the way. If he refuses to accept the lies from the devil, he can be sure nothing can keep him from becoming the person I made him to be. He can accomplish anything I have planned for his life.

"He is my special little man chosen for greatness and filled with my ability and power. Tell him that!"

When I finished reading the prophecy, Zeke's face was radiant. Strongholds the devil had built up in his young mind had been broken. Our precious grandson was finally free from those evil, destructive lies that had wrapped their tentacles around his soul. The truth had set him free! Because Zeke was so different from his brothers and he so desperately wanted to do everything right, I'm convinced that six-year-old boy didn't like himself very much; therefore, he was convinced no one else loved him either— not even God.

The next day after I gave the dog to Zeke, his mother asked him if he liked his puppy. He said, "Mom, this puppy is my *life!* God gave it to me. We can't treat it like just any other toy. We have to take good care of it."

And he did. Over the next few years, you never saw Zeke without the puppy in his hand. He carried it with him everywhere. It was as much a part of him as his arm or leg. On more than one occasion, Spike, (the puppy's name) got lost or left somewhere, and Zeke cried for him every night. When that happened, we prayed fervently that the dog would be found, and he always was. I think there was a special angel patrol assigned to keep track of Spike and locate him every time.

God knew all along how imaginative Zeke was. He made him that way, so he understood how much a simple stuffed animal would mean to our grandson. Spike got all scruffy and dirty from being handled and dragged from place to place. One time, I had to sew his nose back on after he had been lost outside for several days, but the truth of God's love and acceptance never became tarnished or ever diminished in Zeke's mind. To this day, Ezekiel has not been prone to bouts of depression. He knows he's forgiven and is settled about who he is and is at peace with how God has made him.

Sadly, there are many who are not so fortunate. The battering hand of life has left them with a shattered, mangled self-image, causing severe dysfunction, especially in relationships. We have learned that the law of human relationship hinges on love, and our ability to love others depends on our ability to love ourselves. Therein lies the problem.

"For the whole Law [concerning human relationships] is complied with in the one precept, You shall love your neighbor as [you do] yourself" (Gal. 5:14; emphasis mine).

How Much Are You Worth?

During our years of ministry, we have found that low self-esteem is one of the biggest problems Christians face in the body of Christ. Of all people, God's children should value themselves the most. John 3:16 states, "God so greatly loved and dearly prized the world that He [even] gave up His only begotten (unique) Son, so that whoever believes in (trusts in, clings to, relies on) Him shall not perish (come to destruction, be lost) but have eternal (everlasting) life."

If you pay $5,000 for a piece of jewelry, how valuable is it to you? In your eyes, it's worth $5,000 or else you would not have paid that much for it. How much do you think Jesus is worth to his Heavenly Father? To answer that, you would probably struggle to find a figure that fits. You wouldn't be able to put a price tag on Jesus. Eventually, you would have to decide he was worth an immeasurable amount to God.

Yet in John 3:16, we learn that God gave Jesus as payment to purchase you from the hand of the enemy so you might become part of his family and inherit eternal life. What does that say about how valuable you are to God? You are not worth just a measly million dollars, or even a billion, or quadrillion. God gave his most priceless possession to buy you back. That makes your value to God immeasurable.

So what is the problem? If we are that precious to God, why are so many of his children stumbling through life, thinking they're trash, feeling inferior and worthless? The answer lies in the fact that we've been contaminated with a negative viewpoint of ourselves sometime in our life and we don't know how to change that image or haven't made the effort to alter how we see ourselves.

How Your Self-image Is Formed

To change how you see yourself, first you must understand how your self-image was formed in the first place. In the beginning, when God created man, he didn't make rubbish. In Genesis 1: 26–27, we learn the opposite is true:

> God said, Let Us [Father, Son, and Holy Spirit] make mankind in Our image, after Our likeness, and let them have complete authority over the fish of the sea, the birds of the air, the [tame] beasts, and over all of the earth, and over everything that creeps upon the earth. So God created man in His own

image, in the image and likeness of God He created him; male and female He created them.

Mankind had an impressive beginning. When God formed man, he fashioned Adam to be just like himself. What God saw when he looked at his own image he placed on the inside of man.

All would have gone the way God planned if only that original image had remained intact inside of Adam and Eve. Unfortunately, that didn't happen. In Genesis 3, we read about the deception instigated by Satan resulting in rebellion on the part of our first parents. When sin entered their lives, it had a shattering effect on the picture God had branded on their inner man, and a devastating effect on the human race as a whole.

The truth is: The me I see, is the me I'll be! How we see ourselves determines the way we react and respond in any given situation. Sin destroys our confidence and causes us to act stupid, irrational, and self-conscious.

After Adam and Eve sinned, they hid from God. When he finally located them, he asked why they had gone into hiding. They admitted they had run away because they were afraid and naked. God then confronted them with the question: "Who told you that you were naked?" (Gen. 3:11).

Up until that time, they had only seen themselves clothed in the image and glory of God, so they hadn't even been naked. It wasn't until their hearts were tainted with sin that the glory departed. That's when they saw themselves differently. The Godlike image that gave them the confidence to take dominion over the earth was shattered. In its place, a distorted view of who they were became imprinted on their inner man. They even had a twisted outlook concerning their relationship with God and tragically lost sight of their mission here on earth. From that time on, instead of Adam and Eve taking charge as planned, even weeds threatened to overpower their labor. They had to sweat to accomplish anything.

Sin causes you to feel flawed; therefore, you become self-conscious, which is the undesirable characteristic that steals confidence. For example, if you arrive at church wearing your best white shirt, and just before you walk through the door, you notice a big blob of ketchup on the front of your shirt from the sandwich you gobbled down as you bolted out the door. You see that ketchup stain perched on your lapel like a red beacon light, screaming "slob," and the entire time you are at church, when you should be mindful of the needs of others, you are self-conscious. Your attention is focused on trying to hide that embarrassing stain. The confidence you should have is shaken, because now, in your eyes, you are blemished.

That's the way a lot of people feel about their self-image. Because we have "all sinned and come short of the glory of God" (Rom. 3:23), we are all in the same boat. Each of us has lost the image of the glory of God that we originally had. As individuals who feel flawed and tarnished, we clutch at something or someone on the outside to make us feel good about ourselves.

God never planned it that way. He intended us to feel good about ourselves because of the image he placed on the inside and then spend the rest of our lives meeting the needs of others. In order to love others as we should, we have to learn to love ourselves in a healthy way.

To do this, you must be convinced you have been cleansed from the pollution of sin, guilt, and shame. You have to get the ketchup off your shirt, so to speak, and then you can think about someone besides yourself. Otherwise, your spirit will be loaded down with guilt, and you will have no ability to focus outwardly. People who are sick very seldom think about how they can help someone else. They're hurting, so their whole concern is to convince others to help them. Likewise, those who are weighed down with guilt ache from that burden also, so their whole center of attention is on getting their needs met.

Because sin always produces guilt, it creates an atmosphere of selfishness in an individual's life causing all kinds of complications.

Symptoms of Guilt and Shame

Guilt is a feeling of heaviness that is an unbearable burden. It causes the spirit of a person to experience depression, making everything seem dark and oppressive. A person who is weighed down with guilt shows signs of lack of energy, and that load of remorse can even make him physically and mentally ill.

It goes without saying that if guilt is not dealt with, it will have the undesirable effect of interfering with a person's fellowship with God. Like Adam and Eve who hid from God, you will find yourself not wanting to spend time in the presence of God or his people. Therefore, guilt leaves you drained of your spiritual energy, causing you to be a weak Christian. That renders you helpless in the face of any new attacks from the enemy, robbing you of the courage to fight back.

Ephesians 6:14 lists the "breastplate of righteousness" as the important item needed to protect your heart during spiritual warfare. If you have guilt in your life, you have lost your sense of righteousness. Consequently, your breastplate has been stripped away, leaving you naked and vulnerable to the enemy. Guilt then causes you to sin even more because you are susceptible to temptation, and so the vicious cycle goes on and on.

There's so much pressure on people who have the negative effects of unresolved guilt and shame that getting along with others is difficult. It's nearly impossible to live under the burden of guilt and still operate in the fruit of the Spirit: love, joy, peace, longsuffering, gentleness, goodness, meekness, faithfulness, and temperance (see Gal. 5:22–23).

Dealing with a Shame-based Nature

Unresolved guilt causes a person to develop a shame-based nature creating a whole new set of long-range, problematic symptoms. Joyce Meyer, in her book *Beauty for Ashes*, defines shame as a deep-seated sense of disappointment in oneself, not on the bases of *what you have done*, but on the basis of *who you are*. She describes a person who has a shame-based nature as one whose outward behavior is demonstrated in these various ways: alienation; compulsive behavior such as drug/alcohol/substance abuse; eating disorders; addiction to money, work, or other objects or activities; sexual perversions; excessive need to be in control; lack of self-control or self-discipline; gossiping; a judgmental spirit; and the whole ugly list goes on and on.

Some other symptoms of a shame-based nature are depression, a deep sense of inferiority—"there is something wrong with me" thinking—a failure syndrome, isolating loneliness, and lack of confidence.

Neurotic behavior, demonstrated by assuming too much responsibility, is also an outgrowth of shame. A neurotic person automatically presumes that he or she is at fault in times of conflict, which can often develop into perfectionism. We know living peaceably with a perfectionist is almost impossible.

Probably the most devastating consequence of shame is the presence of an underlying sense of timidity and fear. Because 1 John 4:18 reads, "Perfect love casts out fear, and he who fears is not yet perfected in love," we can assume, where fear exists, love does not abound. Because the law of love is the law governing all relationships, a fear-filled person constantly breaks that important law. Consequently, building solid relationships becomes virtually impossible.

The Proper Way to Be Delivered from Guilt and Shame

The human race would be in a terrible state if there was not an effective way to deal with sin and its devastating consequences. In the Old Testament, because each person did what was right in his own eyes, sin thrived, and at one point, conditions had gotten so bad God contemplated wiping mankind off the face of the earth with a flood. He didn't do it, however. One family was saved because God gave them detailed instructions for building an ark, which became their salvation.

The effects of sin are always chaotic and destructive, especially to relationships. Just like the ark God made available for Noah in the early days of creation, today, God has made a wonderful way to escape the devastation that sin brings into our lives.

I like to put the process of deliverance from sin in a neat little nutshell: just admit it, and quit it! Thorough cleansing from the effects of guilt comes only through sincere and heartfelt repentance. Repentance is not just a half-hearted confession of wrongdoing when we get caught; it goes far deeper than that. Mark 6:12, from the Amplified Bible, describes a broader view of repentance: "So they went out and preached that men should repent (that they should change their minds for the better and heartily amend their ways, with abhorrence of their past sins)."

True repentance doesn't mean a sinner just confesses his sins. It includes changing his mind and ways, then turning from and abhorring sin. A truly repentant person will experience sorrow or grief for the sins he has committed. Second Corinthians 7:10 talks about two different kinds of grief—one that leads to salvation, and the other breeding death:

> For godly grief and the pain God is permitted to direct, produce a repentance that leads and contributes to salvation and deliverance from evil, and it never brings regret; but worldly grief [the hopeless sorrow that is characteristic of the pagan world] is deadly—breeding and ending in death.

The difference between godly grief and worldly grief is in what you hate. Godly grief hates *the sin*, causing a person to turn from it in abhorrence. On the other hand, worldly grief drives an individual to hate *themselves* for sinning, resulting in a deep-seated sense of shame, which is the breeding ground for destruction.

Those two kinds of grief were dramatized in Peter's life after he denied Jesus three times and in Judas's life following his betrayal of Jesus. Peter, after the last cock-crowing episode, "went out and wept bitterly [that is, with painfully moving grief]" (Luke 22:62). Judas, on the other hand based his repentance on self-hatred because of what he had done. Instead of repenting to God, what little remorse he had was directed toward men who could care less:

"When Judas, His betrayer, saw that [Jesus] was condemned, [Judas was afflicted in mind and troubled for his former folly; and] with remorse (with little more than a selfish dread of the consequences) he brought back the thirty pieces of silver to the chief priests and the elders, Saying, I have sinned in betraying innocent blood. They replied, 'What is that to us? See to that yourself.' And casting the pieces of silver [forward] into the Holy Place of the sanctuary of the temple, he departed; and he went off and hanged himself. (Matt. 27:3–5)"

There are constructive and destructive ways to deal with sin. One will cleanse you from negative effects and the other festers and tarnishes your perspective until your self-image hangs itself.

The Bible reveals the solution to the devastating results of guilt and shame. Because of Jesus's death and the blood he shed, every sin has technically been forgiven long before you ever committed it. When you repent, God is not sitting in heaven trying to decide whether or not you are worthy of his forgiveness. No. When Jesus died and paid for every sin, God's forgiveness was determined beforehand. Now, it is up to you to receive what has already so graciously been provided.

The psalmist spelled it out in chapter thirty-two, verse five: "I acknowledged my sin to You, and my iniquity I did not hide. I said, I will confess my transgressions to the Lord [continually unfolding the past till all is told]—then You [instantly] forgave me the guilt and iniquity of my sin."

Cleansing from Sexual Sins

The most debilitating sins we have encountered during our years of ministry are the effects of sexual sins, especially when experienced during childhood. Satan would like nothing better than to take a beautiful child with the promise of a great destiny and mess up that child for life through sexual abuse and sexual sins. That's why there's an epidemic of sexual exploitation among children today. Kids by the thousands are coming into adulthood dysfunctional and warped in their inner man, and unless it is dealt with properly, sooner or later it causes disaster in relationships. There is a way for a person to be purified from the contaminating effects of molestation.

Because a simple "God, forgive me" prayer doesn't seem to go to the heart of the problem in severe cases, a more in-depth cleansing prayer is needed. A prayer that not only deals with guilt and shame associated with illegitimate sexual activity but also addresses the demons that took advantage of the situation and enforced their devilish lies into the conscious and subconscious nature of a person.

Because sex is the one act that puts humans in a special category with God—one that has the potential to create life—God in his wisdom confined that unique act to marriage. It was designed to safeguard the impressionable psyche of a person in a committed, sheltered relationship. However, when sex is brought out from the confines of that protected environment, it's a different story.

When God laid down laws for the children of Israel in the Old Testament, especially in Leviticus 18, he went into great detail concerning who they were not to have sex with. Sprinkled throughout his commands were these words: "When you have sex with that particular individual, you have *uncovered their nakedness.*" That could refer to the physical condition of being naked, but I think God wanted to warn us that when people have sex without his sanction, they become vulnerable.

We never open the door of our house during the summer with the intention of letting the flies inside; however, when the door is open, those pesky insects are poised and ready to take advantage of the opening and sail in, totally uninvited. The devil is that way too. He has nasty little demons nosing around looking for an open door determined to get in to torment and ultimately mess up a person's life.

Satan likes to deceive people into thinking that messing around with sex is harmless, but underneath it all, his demons are ready to take advantage of any open doors. They swarm in, injecting their poisonous, shame-based venom into the self-image of unsuspecting individuals. Consequently, those infected are prone to go through life feeling tainted and flawed without really knowing the reason why.

Over the years, having counseled many who have that problem, the Lord led me to compile a cleansing prayer addressing the various components of sexual sins. One lady danced into the room the next day after going through this prayer, announcing she felt like a new woman. Before, she had been despondent, but that day, she was radiant. Many have reported that as a result of this prayer, their ability to relate to their spouse drastically improved. They were not so touchy or easily offended because of experiencing a new sense of security that had not been there before.

Cleansing Prayer:

1. Ask God to *forgive you* for your part in the incident. The problem with most victims of abuse is a nagging sense of guilt about the incident even if they were victims, thinking they might have had something to do with causing it. Repentance is the only remedy for guilt, spiritually speaking, and has the ability to wipe out any remnants of shame. If we skip this part the cleansing would not be complete. However, most who would be using this prayer are individuals who were consensual in the episode.

2. Tell God *you forgive* the other person for what they did to you.

3. *Ask God to forgive* the other individual who was involved in the sin.

4. Take authority over any demon spirits that took advantage of you at the time of the sexual encounter and command them to leave in Jesus's name.

5. Break *every soul tie* that was formed during the incident.

6. Then, praise and thank God you are forgiven and cleansed from the pollution of that sin.

7. Declare you are free; and never let Satan harass you with shame, guilt, or condemnation about it again.

This prayer is most effective when you address each separate sexual encounter. However, if there have been so many incidents that it would be impossible to address individual occurrences one by one, then they could be lumped together according to location or year or any other form of identification so you can be assured that each and every encounter has been dealt with completely. The prayer can be prayed in the presence of a counselor or in private. Each is equally effective.

Soul Ties

As you read through the prayer, you might not be familiar with the term "soul ties." When God invented sex, he had in mind two individuals coming together and becoming one. That's why he so strongly commanded sex to be practiced only in the confines of the committed institution of marriage. Sex not only causes two people to be united in the physical sense; but during this vulnerable act, the soul—the mind, will, and emotions—of a person becomes tightly entwined with the other partner, developing what is called "soul ties."

It's like gluing two pieces of different colored construction paper together. When you try to tear them apart later, both pieces of paper will be hopelessly ripped, and some of each color stays tightly glued to the other.

That's what happens in your soul during casual or promiscuous sexual encounters. Your emotions become completely wrapped around that other person; and you can go through life fragmented, never making the connection. God says that when a couple gets married, they become merged into one. Does a marriage ceremony in a church make that happen? No. They are then married in the eyes of God and the law, but there has been no union yet. When they have sex, that's when the two become one, but not just physically; it's much, much more than that.

When two people have sex, specific hormones are released that affect the brain. These hormones are:

- Epinephrine and Norepinephrine—they are the hormones that cause a psychological and chemical bonding. In the body, epinephrine causes the fight or flight response, and norepinephrine intensifies the experience. That's what happens in the body. In the brain, there's a psychological and chemical bonding to that person. Have you ever wondered why women continue to stay with a man who is abusive? A big part of it is because she has experienced a psychological and chemical bonding with that man, so leaving is incredibly difficult and often doesn't happen without someone from the outside intervening.

- Oxytocin—causes imprinting in the brain. Oxytocin is present in the brain when a mother nurses her baby. Nursing releases oxytocin in the brain of both mother and child. Thus, that child is imprinted in the mother's brain and the mother is imprinted in the child's brain. There's an incredible bonding that takes place between mother and child. Very recently, medical science has discovered that when two people have sex, oxytocin is released in the brains of both partners. You know what that means? It means that the man and the woman are imprinted on one another.

If you have been ripped apart as a result of illicit sex, to become a whole person again in the soulish realm cannot be accomplished with the help of psychology alone. Without supernatural help, the outlook is pretty bleak. However, the God who made you has the ability to remake any vessel who returns to the potter's wheel. His power can cleanse and untangle any web the enemy has woven in your life.

After you have prayed the cleansing prayer, having made a conscious effort to deal with any areas of guilt or shame in your life, now you are ready to start rebuilding your self-image, reshaping it into the original pattern God designed for you.

4

Mirror, Mirror on the Wall

Have you ever seen your own face? If I asked you that question, you would probably say, "Of course. I know what I look like." But have you seen your own face? If you are truthful your answer would be "no." You know what you look like only because you have used a mirror or something that reflected back the image you are so familiar with. You can't see your face without the help of some outward device.

That's the way you developed your inward picture as well. Your self-image has developed over the years by looking into mirrors held up by people or circumstances reflecting back their view of you. There are many mirrors you look into during your life that affect your self-image. The most common is the mirror held by your parents. What they said about you and how they treated you has the greatest impact on how a child sees himself. If you have been told consistently you are lazy, worthless, ugly, or rebellious—and the list goes on and on—that image has been chiseled into your inner man, causing corresponding behavior to become embedded in your thought patterns and belief system.

"As a man thinketh in his heart, so is he" (Prov. 23:7, KJV).

In my house, there are two mirrors I use most often. One is the sliding door on our bathtub and the other on our dresser in the bedroom. The bathtub mirror makes me look ten pounds heavier than the one on the dresser. That's most unfortunate because generally, when I look in the mirror on the tub, I have just finished taking a bath or shower, and—well, you get the picture.

It's up to me to decide which mirror is telling the truth. One mirror is distorted and the other probably accurate, but I don't know which is which. I have to choose the one I believe to be correct. On my good days, I pick the mirror on the dresser because it makes me feel better about myself. But should I ever throw a pity party, I can wallow in negative feedback by studying my reflection in the tub mirror, and the party's on.

Negative feedback not only affects how you see yourself, but ultimately, it shapes your destiny. The children of Israel experienced a spectacular deliverance from four hundred years of slavery in Egypt, but when they approached the land promised them, the first challenge they faced were giants. Everything would have been all right if they had not looked in the mirror those men of huge stature held up for them to see. Instead, they did what a lot of us do; they formed their opinion of *who they were* based on comparison. In Numbers 13:31–33 they cried:

> "We are not able to go up against the people [of Canaan], for they are stronger than we are." So they brought the Israelites an evil report of the land which they had scouted out, saying, "The land through which we went to spy it out is a land that devours its inhabitants. And all the people that we saw in it are men of great stature. There we saw the Nephilim [or giants], the sons of Anak, who come from the giants; *and we were in our own sight as grasshoppers, and so we were in their sight.*" (emphasis mine)

The ten spies saw the staggering size of the giants and decided they were like grasshoppers compared to them. Not only did they let that mirror intimidate them, but because of what they saw, they became convinced they couldn't conquer the inhabitants of the land. Their self-image became so devalued that they didn't see themselves as men any longer but only as pathetic little insects.

A Certified Mirror

If the mirrors you look at are so important to your inner image, then it's imperative you find a mirror that tells the truth. A certified mirror, if you will. Have you ever been in a fun house or some type of amusement facility where there is a room filled with mirrors? Each mirror has a particular way it perverts how you really look. Some make you look fat—like the mirror on my tub, only more so. Others distort different parts of your body presenting a grotesque picture, which is supposed to be funny. You chuckle at what you see because you know those mirrors are not telling the truth. You're aware the image reflected is really a lie, so you laugh it off and go your merry way.

The mirrors of life might not be quite so easy to shrug off as being untrue. In fact, more often than not, you are prone to internalize what others say about you and agree with the picture they paint. As a result, that incorrect image is woven into your belief system as a real portrayal of who you are. So that's who you think you are.

What if those distorted fun house mirrors were the only ones you looked at every day? They would convince you that what you see is what you are, so your self-image would be terribly misrepresented.

That's what many people face in their lives. They have been told consistently they won't amount to anything or, because of abuse, have decided they're worthless and therefore live a life of shame. Consequently, the personality God gave them never emerges, and they fail to fulfill the destiny he placed them on this earth to accomplish.

God never made anyone to be junk. The psalmist said in Psalms 139:13, "For You did form my inward parts; You did knit me together in my mother's womb."

Since each child has been carefully crafted by the Almighty as someone who is valuable and special, a poor self-image is not from God. It's the faulty reflections of life that have successfully altered that view.

How to Reform Your Self-image

What you need is a mirror that has been officially verified as accurate. If every mirror you have seen throughout your lifetime is questionable, is there even one genuine mirror you can depend on to tell you the truth? Thankfully, there is. You find it in 2 Corinthians 3:18:

> And all of us, as with unveiled face, [because we] continued to behold [in the Word of God] as in a mirror the glory of the Lord, are constantly being transfigured into His very own image in ever increasing splendor and from one degree of glory to another; [for this comes] from the Lord [Who is] the Spirit.

The mirror Paul describes reflecting the glory of God is the Word of God. When you look into a physical mirror, whose reflection do you see? If you're the one looking at your reflection, you will see you, not someone else. So if you're looking into the mirror of the Word of God and beholding something glorious staring back at you, who are you seeing? You're looking at your own glorious self.

God's word is the only certified mirror qualified to tell you the truth about who you really are. Jesus announced in John 8:32: "And you will know the Truth, and the Truth will make you free." If the truth makes you free, then what will you be free from? You will be free from the effects of Satan's lies that have wrapped themselves around your inner man creating a stranglehold of insecurity and powerlessness.

The glory that was savagely ripped from the human race when our first parents sinned has once again been offered to those who will accept God's plan of redemption. God gave mankind dominion and intended that we rule and reign with him. That plan was tragically overpowered by a relentless task master who, in turn, dominated mankind, bringing them into a life of hopeless slavery. But God provided a way for everyone to be set free. That's what salvation is all about.

A Cinderella Story

The plan of redemption is much like one of my favorite fairy tales, Cinderella. In the story, Cinderella's wicked stepmother and evil stepsisters dominated her. She became their slave through no fault of her own. Her father had made an unwise choice in marriage (for whatever reason), and then had the audacity to die, leaving Cinderella in the deplorable situation we find her when the story begins. Practically everyone knows the details of that fascinating tale, but to summarize it: The prince was looking for a bride, so he threw a gala event inviting every unmarried maiden in the realm to a magnificent ball. Cinderella's wicked stepsisters went, leaving Cinderella at home without any hope of getting to go, let alone ever having the opportunity to meet the prince.

However, we're delighted when a fairy godmother appears and fixes Cinderella up—complete with a splendid dress, a coach made from a pumpkin, horses from mice, etc. When the festive evening begins at the palace, Cinderella arrives in all her finery and catches the eye of the prince. He falls in love with her at first sight. However, when midnight rolls around, she has to leave abruptly because everything goes back to normal at the stroke of midnight.

In the end, the prince finally finds Cinderella again. They get married and live happily ever after. That's where the fairy tale ends, but that's where my story, or should I say, where the Bible analogy begins. What if the next day, after the wedding, the wicked stepmother and the wretched stepsisters show up at the palace and knock on Cinderella's bedroom door? That despicable crew whines and demands that Cinderella come back home to fix their breakfast, scrub their floors, and do their laundry, just as she has done in the past?

Whether Cinderella gives in to their demands will be determined by the image she currently has of herself. If she still sees herself as a slave, she will go submissively back into a life of obedience under their control and never rule and reign as she has the opportunity to do. However, if she identifies with her role of being a princess instead of a slave, she can exert the authority she has acquired by virtue of her union with the prince. She will drive those wicked people out of her life in the name of the prince because she has been given his name and has all the rights he has. Her behavior will be based on how she sees herself.

Your actions and reactions toward people and situations are determined by how you see yourself. According to the

Bible, if you have been born again, you should see yourself as one who has authority with a commission to rule and reign. You will be happy to know the Cinderella story is in the Bible in Ephesians 2:1–6:

> And you [He made alive], when you were dead (slain) by [your] trespasses and sins. In which at one time you walked [habitually]. You were following the course and fashion of this world [were under the sway of the tendency of this present age], following the prince of the power of the air. [You were obedient to and under the control of] the [demon] spirit that still constantly works in the sons of disobedience [the careless, the rebellious, and the unbelieving, who go against the purposes of God].
>
> Among these we as well as you once lived and conducted ourselves in the passions of our flesh [our behavior governed by our corrupt and sensual nature], obeying the impulses of the flesh and the thoughts of the mind [our cravings dictated by our senses and our dark imaginings]. We were then by nature children of [God's] wrath and heirs of [His] indignation, like the rest of mankind.
>
> But God—so rich is He in His mercy! Because of and in order to satisfy the great and wonderful and intense love with which He loved us, Even when we were dead (slain) by [our own] shortcomings and trespasses, He made us alive together in fellowship and in union with Christ; [He gave us the very life of Christ Himself, the same new life with which He quickened Him, for] it is by grace (His favor and mercy which you did not deserve) that you are saved (delivered from judgment and made partakers of Christ's salvation).

> And He raised us up together with Him and made
> us sit down together [giving us joint seating with
> Him] in the heavenly sphere [by virtue of our being]
> in Christ Jesus (the Messiah, the Anointed One).

That's God's Cinderella story. We were all slaves under the dominion of the devil and his demons, without hope, destined to a life of drudgery and pain. But God—God was so rich in his mercy and loved us so much that he made provision for us to come into union with his son. Once that takes place, we are no longer under the control of the prince of darkness but can rule and reign with Christ seated with him on his throne in heavenly places next to God himself.

In addition, we have Jesus' name bestowed on us. All his authority is ours because we are joint heirs with him, plus everything Jesus has belongs to us.

When I married my husband, all his belongings became mine, including his 1958 Chevrolet Bel Air. I dropped my last name and took his, giving me access to his bank account and credit cards (although back in those days, there was no such thing as a credit card). Nevertheless, what was his became mine. I thought it was a pretty good deal then, and I still do.

Since the biblical Cinderella story is not just a fairy tale but absolute truth, how should we see ourselves? Satan has his mirrors, but God also has a mirror. Just like those two mirrors in my house, I have to choose which one I'm going to believe. You have that choice as well. Are you going to believe those distorted mirrors the devil flashes in front of you, furnished by people and circumstances he uses to convince you of failure and inadequacy in life? Or are you going to look into the mirror of the Word of God and get your glory back? It's your choice.

Jesus showed us how it was done in John 8:13–18. In verse twelve, he had just announced he was the light of the world when the Pharisees reprimanded him for saying such a thing about himself. They insisted in verse thirteen: "You are testifying on your own behalf; Your testimony is not valid and is worthless."

They didn't appreciate how he saw himself, or accept what he said about himself. I like what Jesus did with the mirror the Pharisees tried to get him to look into.

"Jesus answered, 'Even if I do testify on My own behalf, My testimony is true and reliable and valid, for I know where I came from and where I am going; but you do not know where I come from or where I am going.

"'You [set yourselves up to] judge according to the flesh (by what you see). [You condemn by external, human standards.] I do not [set Myself up to] judge or condemn or sentence anyone.'"

He smashed their mirror to pieces. He told them, "I know who I am and where I am headed. You don't have the right to tell me who I am or where I am going because you judge by the flesh, by what you see, and that's not where I get my information." He continued in the following verses to explain where he got his information about who he was:

> Yet even if I do judge, My judgment is true [My decision is right]; for I am not alone [in making it], but [there are two of Us] I and the Father, Who sent Me. In your [own] Law it is written that the testimony (evidence) of two persons is reliable and valid.
>
> I am One [of the Two] bearing testimony concerning Myself; and My Father, Who sent Me, He also testifies about Me. (John 8:16–18)

Jesus knew which mirror was the certified one. First, he found out what the Father said about him, and then he testified of the same thing. In doing so, he saw himself the way his Father viewed him, and that's the only mirror he allowed to influence his life. That empowered him to fulfill to the letter what God sent him into the world to accomplish.

What does all this have to do with relationships? In the previous two chapters we established that there is only one law that governs human relationships: love others as you love yourself. If the way you love others is based on how you love yourself, any discrepancy in the love you have for yourself must be addressed first before you can successfully love others.

If mirrors from your past have shut down your ability to love yourself, there is another remarkable mirror that tells you the honest truth about who you are. In order to reform and repair your self-image, it must be the only mirror you allow in your life.

Here is that extraordinary mirror. If you consistently take the truths of these scriptures, speaking them out loud on a regular basis, the lies formed from a lifetime of abuse will fade away in light of truth.

Who Am I?

I am God's own handiwork (his workmanship), recreated to do good works, living the good life which he prearranged and made ready for me to live (see Eph. 2:10).

I am a new creature in Christ, old things have passed away, and all things have become new (see 2 Cor. 5:17).

I am the temple of God. The Spirit of God dwells in me (see 1 Cor. 3:16).

I have the thoughts, feelings, and purposes of Jesus (see 1 Cor. 2:16).

I have been bought with a great price; therefore, I will glorify God in my body and my spirit (see 1 Cor. 6:20).

I am a member of Christ's body (see 1 Cor. 6:15).

I have been made more than a conqueror through Christ (see Rom. 8:37).

Nothing can separate me from God's love (see Rom. 8:38–39).

Sin has no power over me (see Rom. 6:14).

The law of life in Christ Jesus has made me free from the law of sin and death (see Rom. 8:2).

I am an able minister of the New Testament (see 2 Cor. 3:6).

I am the righteousness of God in Jesus Christ, and I reign in life as a king (see 2 Cor. 5:21; Rom. 5:17).

I am a child of God through Jesus Christ, and a joint heir with Christ (see Rom. 8:16–17).

I have been accepted into the beloved family of God (see Eph. 1:6).

Because I am the temple of God, God dwells in me and walks in me (see 2 Cor. 6:16).

I have been predestined to become just like Jesus (see Rom. 8:29).

Because I am in Jesus Christ, I am Abraham's seed; therefore, I am heir of the world (see Gal. 3:29; Rom. 4:13).

I have been blessed with all spiritual blessings (see Eph. 1:3).

God is for me; therefore, no one can be against me (see Rom. 8:31).

I am chosen of God so that I can become holy and without blame before him in love (see Eph. 1:4).

I have put off my former life, which was full of corruption and deceitful lusts, and have put on a new life, which is created in righteousness and true holiness (see Eph. 4:22–24).

I am confident that Jesus Christ will complete the good work that he has started in me (see Phil. 1:6).

I can do all things through Christ which strengtheneth me (see Phil. 4:13).

I am complete in Jesus Christ (see Col. 2:10).

God is at work in me, creating the power, and the desire, to will and to work for his good pleasure, satisfaction, and delight (see Phil. 2:13).

I have been delivered from the power of darkness and have been translated into the kingdom of Jesus Christ (see Col. 1:13).

The blood of Jesus has cleansed me, so I am holy, blameless, and unreprovable in God's sight (see Col. 1:22).

I have put off the old image of anger, wrath, malice, blasphemy, lying, and filthy communication, and have put on the new image—the image of Christ (see Col. 3:8–10).

I am the elect of God, holy and beloved of God, so therefore, I put on bowels of mercies, kindness, humbleness of mind, meekness, longsuffering, forgiveness, and love, which is the bond of perfectness (see Col. 3:12–14).

God has not given me a spirit of fear, but of power, love, and a sound mind (see 2 Tim. 1:7).

Now that you know who you are and can properly love yourself, you are ready to deal with any faulty, destructive habits that have a tendency to trouble your relationships.

If you have never accepted Jesus as your savior, or are not sure you are born again, it will be difficult to walk in the love required for healthy relationships. You must have God's love deposited in your heart to be successful. He has made it as easy as praying a heartfelt prayer that moves you out of the kingdom of darkness and deposits you into his family—the kingdom of light.

> [*The Father*] has delivered and drawn us to Himself out of the control and the dominion of darkness and has transferred us into the kingdom of the Son of His love, in Whom we have our redemption through His blood, [*which means*] the forgiveness of our sins. (Col. 1:13–14)

Your confession determines your position in spiritual things. Paul revealed the steps you need to take in order to be saved, or born again in Romans 10: 9–10:

> Because if you acknowledge and confess with your lips that Jesus is Lord and in your heart believe that God raised Him from the dead, you will be saved.
> For with the heart a person believes (adheres to, trusts in, and relies on Christ) and so is justified (declared righteous, acceptable to God), and with the mouth he confesses (declares openly and speaks out freely his faith) and confirms [*his*] salvation.

If you have never been born again and would like to enjoy all the benefits of a life of peace through Jesus Christ, pray this prayer:

Dear Heavenly Father,
I acknowledge I am a sinner and need to be set free from guilt and shame that are a result of sin. I believe Jesus came to Earth and died for my sins and then rose again, and now every sin I have ever committed has been paid for. I accept

Jesus Christ as my Savior and receive him as my Lord. I am now a new creature in Christ. I am through with my old life and have a new life in Jesus. I will serve him the rest of my days. Thank you, Lord. I am now born again and part of the family of God.

If you just prayed that prayer for the first time, welcome to the family!

5

The Law of Human Obligations

The day is perfect. The sun places its stamp of approval on the occasion as it kisses the environment with its inviting warmth. The church is decorated to perfection with the soft glow of candlelight creating an atmosphere of romance. Melodious strains of a love song fill the air while graceful bridesmaids glide down the aisle decked out in elegant wedding finery. A hush fills the crowded sanctuary as the groom takes his place, standing stately and handsome, meticulously dressed in his white tuxedo. Then, the anticipated moment arrives. The rear doors slowly open to reveal the radiant bride in all her glory. The glowing vision of loveliness begins her measured procession into the waiting arms of her eager bridegroom. When the "I dos" are said and all the promises made to each other, witnesses of this lovely ceremony leave with sighs of approval, delighted that the two lovers have officially become husband and wife.

We have witnessed a beautiful picture of two people entering into the marriage relationship with wonderful expectations of great marital bliss. Unfortunately, the happiness most couples are thinking about when they get married is not how to make their newly acquired spouse happy but thinking about *their own gratification*, anticipating how the other person can make them happy, fulfilled, and complete, instead of how they can please their mate.

Amid all this glorious wedding to do, if we could go beneath the beautiful wedding dress and the fashionable tux and unzip each of the marriage partners, more than likely, we would find an internal list engraved on the inside of each one itemizing what the other must do to make them happy. This internal catalog is called the law of human obligations. Most people have one if they are in any type of relationship. In reality, this file has been formulated from various ideals collected little by little from many sources throughout the formative years.

This list does involve the law of love, all right, which is the main law governing relationships; however, you expect the *other* person to fulfill that law in order to demonstrate their love for *you*. Certainly, it's enjoyable when someone close to you consistently exhibits the traits of love toward you. Therefore, you might have a tendency to apply unusual pressure to try to get the other person to always walk in love on your behalf. However, when you endeavor to enforce that law in another person's life, you are *no longer* keeping the law of love yourself, but it has become your law of human obligations.

The law of love is *your* law, not one you are authorized to impose on someone else. Because we're all born selfish, we come into this world with a factory-installed list of human obligations already intact, and then we build on it year after year as we mature. Most demands we place on others stem from just a few fixed thought patterns or paradigms originating from our embedded selfish nature. Some examples are:

You must always treat me the way I want to be treated.

You must always be sensitive to my needs.

You must never inconvenience me.

You must do *what* I want, *when* I want, *in the way* I want it done.

In order to change a relationship, you must first change your paradigm of life. A paradigm is the way you view and interpret the world in general. It's the set of eyeglasses you look through to determine how you are going to analyze or decide in a given situation. To change in any area, you have to change the way you think. In other words, to actually change any relationship, you need to tear up your internal list.

Who's in Control?

It is the tendency of human nature to want to control someone else. That's no big surprise because in the beginning, when God created man, he gave him a commission to take dominion. Because we have been authorized to dominate, there is an internal urge to want to perfect and correct at will. However, God never expected us to manage a situation apart from his power. When sin entered the human race, mankind began to endeavor to do it on his own, and that's when major problems arose.

When we find ourselves in an unpleasant situation, we naturally get ready to dominate. However, apart from God, we invariably use *improper* means for taking dominion. Those ways are through intimidation, domination, and manipulation.

Anger, ill-temper, bad moods, or harsh, cutting speech are some ways intimidation is enforced. A person who uses those methods to control is saying, "If you don't do what I want you to do, it's going to get ugly." So in order to avoid the pain of another confrontation of that type, the other individual usually lives in fear that they are going to upset the more aggressive one. Thus, an atmosphere of intimidation is created while one person dominates and the other is controlled.

Another subtler form of control is domineering. This type of person is bossy and overbearing, and usually critical and picky.

An even less obvious form, and perhaps the most used, is manipulation. Even though it may not be as apparent, it's quite effective and just as destructive. A person can manipulate by pouting, withdrawing attention or affection, making the other person feel guilty, and—I'm sorry to say—by utilizing tears. We woman are pretty good at most of those, especially crying.

I'm not referring to the tears we shed when we're hurt or sorrowful, or even those that come when we experience PMS or have menopausal symptoms. Manipulative tears are the calculated ones with the intention of motivating the other person to some type of action. I don't want to insinuate that women are the only ones who use those tactics of manipulation. Men do it as well, in their own masculine way.

Intimidation, domination, and manipulation are illegitimate means of managing our relationships. In fact, most relationship problems arise because one or both partners have chosen their favorite way to control based on their personality and work it to the max.

The apostle John has a pretty stern revelation about anyone who doesn't keep the laws of God including the law of love. He calls it sin.

In 1 John 3:4 he writes, "Everyone who commits (practices) sin is guilty of lawlessness; for [that is what] sin is, lawlessness (the breaking, violating of God's law by transgression or neglect—being unrestrained and unregulated by His commands and His will)."

God's laws are there in order to regulate and restrain your behavior, and it's your responsibility to put them into practice in your life, not so you can implement them in someone else's life. You may have noticed that when you make an effort to enforce one of your laws in someone else's life, it never seems to work. In fact, the more you harp, the more ingrained their bad behavior becomes. So what's the deal?

If a person tries to keep laws that are enforced from the *outside* only, and are not *in their heart,* they are doomed to fail from the start. Paul addressed this dilemma in Romans 7. He lamented that even though he really wanted to do what was right, everything he was supposed to do he wound up not doing. On the other hand, what he found himself doing were the very things he wasn't supposed to do. Finally in verse twenty-four, he cried out in frustration, "O unhappy and pitiable and wretched man that I am."

That's the way we feel when we try to keep someone else's laws that are not in our own heart. However, before the seventh chapter of Romans ends, Paul has finally found the solution to his predicament. He wraps it up by saying that because of Jesus, now he can keep the laws, because they are in his heart and not just an outward set of rules that he is forced to adhere to.

Paul discovered the laws you can keep successfully are the ones you have internalized and have become a standard for your life, not the laws imposed on you from somebody else. You keep those inner laws because you *want to*, not because you *have to*.

God knew this and was well aware that the Old Testament laws could never be enforced effectively; that's why Jesus had to come and establish a new covenant.

> "For this is the covenant that I will make with the house of Israel after those days," says the Lord: "I will imprint My laws upon their minds, even upon their innermost thoughts and understanding, and engrave them upon their hearts; and I will be their God, and they shall be My people." (Heb. 8:10)

That's why your well-constructed laws of human obligations will never change the behavior of anyone. They are *your laws* and not theirs. Without a heart change, all their good intentions will not give them the ability to carry them out.

To be successful in any relationship, it's important to *never* put demands on other people to meet your needs. At every point of expectation, there is a potential for disappointment. When you make the decision to release everyone, your spouse included, from any further obligation to make you happy, content, or satisfied, you cut out a lot of frustration and hurt in your life. Consequently, you won't have the task of having to constantly deal with disappointment after disappointment.

Sowing and Reaping

If you can't demand or manipulate and still be obedient to God's law, are you just stuck in a bad relationship with nothing you're allowed to do to change it? Good question, and certainly an understandable one. No one likes to endure the conflicts of an unhappy relationship and feel there's no way out.

There is a way you can initiate a welcome change in any situation apart from improper dominion. A wonderful law woven throughout the entire Bible unfolds God's way to implement change in any realm. It's called the law of sowing and reaping. It is written down in regard to relationships in Luke 6:31: "And as you would like and desire that men would do to you, do exactly so to them."

You may recognize that scripture as the "golden rule," but it's much more than just a nice sounding Sunday school memory verse. It represents a powerful way to release God's life-changing ability into the behavior of another person.

Jesus explains it even further in Luke 6:32: "If you [merely] love those who love you, what quality of credit and thanks is that to you? *For even the [very] sinners love their lovers (those who love them).*" (emphasis mine)

Even the most disobedient, ornery person will return love to the individual who loves them first. If you can find some way to genuinely love the person who troubles your relationship, then you can sow into their lives the love you want to reap, and instead of demanding they love you, watch them change.

It's All About the King

The account of Queen Esther has always intrigued me. She was a nobody from an oppressed race of people in a foreign land, yet she rose to have such extraordinary influence that she changed the destiny of an entire nation.

The king of that ancient civilization was one of the most powerful rulers during that period of time. At the flick of his finger, he could order someone beheaded based only on his momentary whim. Certainly, he was a man to be feared and respected. To approach or cross such a royal leader would have to be done with a great deal of trepidation, yet his reigning queen, Vashti, did just that. She refused to come to his imperial banquet when she was summoned, so Vashti was banned from the kingdom and removed from her position as queen.

King Xerxes then had all the beautiful maidens of the land brought to the palace to find a queen replacement. Among those selected was Esther, a young Jewish girl. I'm sure she had heard stories about this severe, even cruel, king. The reports of his many romantic liaisons were no secret either. He kept a rather large harem on hand to be at his beckoning call, so obviously, he was no novice in that area either. Esther faced a challenge unprecedented in history as she prepared to compete for the position of queen amid the other contenders.

What must have gone through her mind during those twelve months of rigorous preparation? One thing she must have known—beauty was not going to be enough. After all, Vashti had been so beautiful the king had sent for her to come to the banquet to display her beauty to "the people and the princes, because she was fair to behold" (Est.1:11).

The search for a new Queen was based on the royal decree that they were to find someone *better* than Vashti. How can you be better than one of the most beautiful women in the world? That was probably one of the disturbing thoughts Esther had to deal with during her waiting period. Tommy Tenney, a Bible scholar and writer of biblical fiction, addressed that dilemma in his book *Hadassah*. He wrote Esther's thoughts this way: "God spoke to me about my challenges ahead. The first words of wisdom that came to me had to do with my upcoming night with the King. 'It is not about you. It is about the King. Focus on him.' And I resolved, in the months ahead, to do just that."

Sometime during those twelve arduous months, Esther learned how to love a wicked king. Esther 2:17 is the key to the whole story. If this verse had not been true, the story would have been vastly different. "And the king loved Esther more than all the women, and she obtained grace and favor in his sight more than all the maidens, so that he set the royal crown on her head and made her queen instead of Vashti."

King Xerxes was looking for someone *better* than Vashti, but instead found someone he could *love!*

How did that happen? This ruler was certainly not noted for his ability to love. How did Esther get an especially wicked sinner to love her? I believe she applied the "golden rule." "And as you would like and desire that men would do to you, do exactly so to them. If you [*merely*] love those who love you, what quality of credit and thanks is that to you? For even the [*very*] sinners love their lovers (those who love them)."

It definitely paid off for her. She made a decision that it was going to be "all about the King." As a result, she was able to influence him to such a degree that laws were changed, a whole race of people was saved from destruction, and in the end, she was given a great deal of authority over the whole realm.

One of the biggest lies the devil tries to sell is that somehow selfishness wins. He attempts to persuade you to believe that it's "all about you"; and there is some merit in criticizing, faultfinding, nagging, and bitterness. He'll try to convince you that if you just point out other people's faults, they will change. The lie embedded in that kind of thinking is the belief that if you can be mean enough, they will love you. That sounds laughable and inconceivable, yet selfish people think that way.

We know we need to be loved and endeavor to get what we desperately need from others. However, when we do that, we generally hit a dead end because when we demand love, we never seem to get it. Eventually, we have to face the fact that to be loved, we must become loveable.

Selfish people are not loveable. When you regulate your life toward the gratification of your own needs, you are self-centered. A person who concentrates on themselves remains severely immature; therefore, their ability to love continues to be stunted.

However, if a person seeks to give love rather than receive it, they become, in the process, loveable and will certainly be loved in return.

Paper Clip Policy

I experienced firsthand this principle while my husband was in Bible school. I worked for a manufacturing company as a receptionist during that time. Because I was directly answerable to the head bookkeeper, I did a lot of secretarial work for him. Right away, I knew there were going to be some major challenges when my boss called me back into his office one morning after I laid some typed papers on his desk.

He furiously waved the stack of papers in the air that I had paper clipped together and said in a surly tone of voice, "I don't want you to ever do this again." I wracked my brain trying to figure out what I had done wrong.

I didn't have to wait long to find out. He pointed dramatically at the paper clip that held the documents together and snapped, "Do you see that the little side of this paper clip is on the top paper? I want the big side up always! Do you understand? I want the big side up!"

I got his point but couldn't understand what the big deal was about his paper clip policy. I left his office boiling on the inside. All I could think about was how stupid and picky he was and how bad I wanted to quit. If I couldn't please him with the paper clips, how could I ever get along with him on the other more important things?

That night, I went home, threw myself on the bed and cried. I begged God to let me quit and find an easier job; but on the inside, I detected a still, small voice I recognized as my Heavenly Father's.

I knew he wasn't going to let me quit. He asked if I would let him show me how he saw my boss. Now when you are talking to God, it is best to cooperate with him, so I agreed to look at my grouchy ole' boss through his eyes.

What I saw was a skinny little man who had spent his life working at a job that was not God's perfect plan for him. He told me, at one time he had considered going into the ministry, but decided against it. Naturally, he had to be miserable inside. On top of that, he was shriveled up from years of chain-smoking, and because he was so cranky, he had no friends and very few people liked him.

As the picture unfolded, I looked at what was going on in the man's life and realized the whole thing was not about me anymore. Something stirred in my heart I recognized as compassion. When I went back to work the next day, I'm convinced my behavior toward my boss remained the same, but evidently because my attitude was different, he sensed the change.

From that day on, he favored me. When others had to beg for their promised raises, I systematically received mine without even asking. He assigned extra hours for me to work when they were available so I could make extra money. When school was over, and my husband and I were preparing to move, he called me into his office and announced he was giving me a bonus. He explained that even though I hadn't worked there a full year, he was still going to give me the equivalent of a week's paid vacation, which was given only to those employees who had been there a year. So it's true. Even a crotchety old bookkeeper will love someone who loves him.

Specks and Beams

When you're being mistreated in a relationship, you may have the tendency to criticize and pass judgment on the offender. Jesus said in Luke 6:41–42 to stop trying to get the speck out of the other person's eye and work on the beam that's in your own. Then, and only then, are you in a position to clearly see the way to remove what's in the other person's eye. Jesus continues his discourse by saying:

> For there is no good (healthy) tree that bears decayed (worthless, stale) fruit, nor on the other hand does a decayed (worthless, sickly) tree bear good fruit. For each tree is known and identified by its own fruit; for figs are not gathered from thornbushes, nor is a cluster of grapes picked from a bramble bush.
>
> The upright (honorable, intrinsically good) man out of the good treasure [*stored*] in his heart produces what is upright (honorable and intrinsically

good), and the evil man out of the evil storehouse brings forth that which is depraved (wicked and intrinsically evil); for out of the abundance (overflow) of the heart his mouth speaks. (Luke 6:43–45)

Have you ever wondered why Jesus followed the profound subject of judging others with a botany lesson? For years, I couldn't make the connection between eye specks and plants until I realized he wasn't talking about trees at all. He was referring to the heart. If there's something *rotten* in the heart, then there will be something *stinking in the attitude.*

Jesus was saying, instead of digging around in the eyes looking for specks to remove, work on the root instead. The eye is not the problem; the root is. You have to change the root of a tree in order to change the fruit. In an individual's life, to successfully change the outgrowth of his behavior, you must first change his heart. But how can a heart be changed?

Most of us have tried to change someone else's behavior at one time or another and failed miserably. If we were wise, we finally gave up and said, "Lord I can't do it anymore. They are in your hands." That's the only way the job will ever get done. God is the only one who has access to the heart of a person, and only he can bring about a true heart change.

First Samuel 16:7 confirms that God doesn't see as man sees: "For man looks on the outward appearance, but the Lord looks on the heart."

Proverbs 21:1 reports, "The King's heart is in the hand of the Lord, as are the watercourses; He turns it whichever way He wills." If a person's heart is going to pivot at all, it will happen because it's in the hands of the Lord.

If ever there was anyone who practiced trying to change someone else's behavior, it was me. Because of my melancholy temperament—the kind that needs all visible ducks in a neat little row—then add on top of that a teaching gift, what you have is an assertive, controlling machine. Over the years, when I repeatedly encountered severe frustration every time I tried to initiate changes in the imperfect people who were part of my life, God arrested me with this revelation: "Your voice is only a human voice that carries with it no power to make changes; it only produces condemnation. My voice is an eternal one, filled with creative power. It has the ability to produce faith, which is the only source of change. My voice produces revelation and growth."

I responded, "God are you trying to tell me the changes I demand from others will only produce a rebellious and defensive reaction if all I do is point out and harp on their faults, and that you are the only one who can make any permanent changes in their hearts?"

I could almost hear God breathe a sigh of relief and whisper, "I think she's finally got it!"

I can't say I have always kept my mouth shut. However, when I revert to doing it my way, and then invariably have to retreat time after time in order to lick my wounds, I finally became convinced God's way was best. I can report there have been some noticeable changes in what looked like impossible situations over the years by simply praying to God, who has access to the hearts of problem people, instead of pounding away with my words. That doesn't mean you can't have honest communication in a relationship, but if the ground work hasn't been laid in prayer, the one you are trying to converse with is likely to receive your self-perceived exposé as criticism rather than the eye-opening revelation you had expected.

If you're serious about finding a cure for an ailing relationship, check your list. What law are you operating from: the law of love or a series of laws based on human obligations? If you find you possess that ominous internal list, destroy it. Make the sensible choice to regulate your life and restrain your behavior by God's commands and his will. Determine to live your life meeting the needs of others; and look out for their interests instead of your own, believing that God will take care of your interests, being fully convinced that what you sow you will surely reap.

6

Offenses Will Come

There is an old folk tale about two porcupines that huddled together trying to keep warm in the middle of a cold Vermont winter. However, they continually had to move apart because even though they *needed* each other, they kept *needling* each other.

In an ideal world, there would never be anyone who would irritate you, but we all know the society we live in is teeming with people who are far from perfect. In fact, Jesus warned us that "offenses would come" (Luke 17:1, kjv).

Very seldom can you go through even one day, let alone a lifetime, without having the opportunity to get offended. You may think getting offended is just one of those unpleasant hazards of life that you can't escape, and it's no big deal. That's not the way the Bible looks at it. God calls getting offended *sin*. The Amplified Bible describes offenses as "temptations (snares, traps set to entice to sin)" (Luke17:1). When those occasions arise and you're faced with offense, it comes with an invitation—an invitation to sin.

The Greek text bears this out by using the word "skandalon" for the word offense, which means "a snare or a trapstick, an occasion to fall, apostasy or displeasure," and it is always referred to as a "stumbling block."

Because offense is designed to cause a person to fall into a trap, it doesn't take a computer geek to figure out the devil is the mastermind behind offense. It's the favorite tool he uses to devastate relationships.

I am familiar with traps because my husband used to trap coyotes. He would set traps for the unsuspecting animal by placing them where he figured the coyote was sure to step but hide them so they were inconspicuous. Then in the immediate proximity of the snare he placed some horrible smelling bait—nasty smelling to us, but evidently quite tempting to the coyote. When the unsuspecting creature snatched the bait, he generally stepped into the trap. That proved most unfortunate for Mr. Coyote because from that moment on his destiny was completely under the control of my husband. Whether he lived or died, ate or drank, or became part of a ladies coat or not was totally dependent on the whim of his captor.

Jesus warned us in John 10:10 that the thief (devil) comes for only one reason: "to steal, kill or destroy." I don't think I would want to take the chance of getting into one of the devil's traps and expect any mercy. Satan would like nothing better than to destroy every relationship you're involved with in order to cause so much misery you determine never to love anyone again. He is busy working his devious plans everywhere: in churches, families, and in every other kind of relationship. Offense is the nasty bait that unsuspecting individuals swallow causing them to get sidetracked from their God-intended destiny; thus, they become the devil's captive. From then on, he controls their fate.

We have established that the law governing relationships is the law of love. When you were born again, your heart was plumbed with love and you can allow it to flow out any time you choose. However, offense is the cruel hand that reaches into the crevices of your heart and turns off your faucet of love, and then you walk around dry and dehydrated all your life living a loveless existence. When the channel of love is turned off, relationships suffer and selfishness takes over. Ultimately, Satan has accomplished what he set out to do: to steal, kill, and destroy.

The Fruit of Offense

I hear this remark often from people who are offended: "No, I'm not offended. I'm just hurt." How do you identify offense for what it really is instead of being blindsided by it and giving it another name?

Offense is probably best identified by its fruit. The Amplified Bible uses some excellent descriptive words to define offense. They are recorded in Matthew 13:21; Mark 4:17; Luke 8:13; and Luke 7:23. A compiled list includes:

- being hurt
- resentful
- annoyed
- repelled
- made to stumble
- withdrawing and standing aloof
- becoming displeased
- indignant
- distrusting and falling away
- deserting him whom you ought to trust and obey

Everyone has most likely contended with some of these characteristics in their lives at one time or another. Whether we like to admit it or not, we have all been offended. Since offense is more than just a little hiccup in the rhythm of life, we should look at it as a devious weapon used by the enemy for the purpose of causing his victim to stumble and fall. It is nothing to play around with and should be avoided at all cost.

If Jesus said offenses were bound to come—and we have found he was right—how can we escape the devastation they bring? When Jesus said we would all have to face the challenge of offense, he didn't imply we had to get offended. Offenses *may* come, but it's *your choice* whether you get offended or not. The trap can be meticulously laid, but you don't have to step into it.

The Big Red Button

Our middle son, Brad, and his wife, Tamy, have an amazing marriage relationship. Even though they are pastors of a great church, and both have been raised around the Word of God most of their lives, they still have had to deal with offense in their marriage just like everyone else. Tamy has shared on several occasions about her battle with offense, and I want to pass on what she learned.

In the early years of their ministry, Brad occasionally irritated her to the max. She then got frustrated because he made her angry, and it always seemed to happen once a month like clockwork—go figure. When he did, she proceeded to tell him "what for" and really gave it to him because she was upset.

If you're familiar with the five love languages, you will remember one of them is "words of affirmation." Well, that's Brad's primary love language, so words are extremely important to him. For a person who has that love language, critical words stab like a knife, and it comes across that you are saying, "I don't love you or care about you." Faultfinding words and a harsh tone of voice are very wounding; so, of course, Brad was terribly hurt each time.

However, Tamy's love language is not "words of affirmation," so she had the habit of just "telling it like it is" and not thinking about it. She said all those hurtful things, not knowing how bad it tore Brad up. As soon as she got through venting, for her, everything was good. She was like, "I'm okay now. Let's kiss and make up."

But Brad was feeling, "Oh my! She just killed me!" It would take him a week to get over it. All the while Tamy was thinking, *What is your problem? I don't get you. Why can't you just snap out of it?*

One day, the Lord gave her a vision. He showed her that down on the inside she had a big red button, and on it was a sign that read: "Caution! Do not touch or there will be an explosion." Then, she saw her husband repeatedly touching that dangerous button. He just kept pushing it over and over again. As she watched the vision, she determined *Well duh! Anyone can see if he pushes the big red button warning him there is going to be an explosion if pushed, then, of course, there is going to be an explosion.*

"Well thank you God for giving me a visual," she said with great relief. Because she had read that if you can give a man a visual, he will then gain understanding and finally get the picture. She couldn't wait to share with Brad that she had this big red button, and if he just wouldn't touch it, there wouldn't be an explosion. And he wouldn't have to be hurt for a week.

Excited that God was so awesome to give her such divine insight, she approached Brad to paint him that great picture. She told him about the big red button, explaining painstakingly that he was not to touch it and patiently pointed out the reason he was getting hurt was because he had been pushing the button. To drive her point home, she explained once again. "You have been touching the big red button, and that's why you are getting hurt. So, from now on, just don't push that button, and you'll not get hurt. And we will be okay," she finished with emphasis.

She thought she had just delivered a great revelation when Brad looked at her and responded emphatically, "You know what? I have a big red button too!"

Tamy thought, *What? This is not about you. This is my revelation.*

Then Brad also pointed out, "Mine also says caution, do not touch or there will be an explosion."

That really got Tamy upset. She had expected there to be this divine understanding come from heaven to Brad, then everything would change, and their relationship forever after would be great.

Finally she got alone with God and was surprised when he gently pointed out, "Now that you see you have a big red button, you need to disengage it."

She responded, "What? I just got this revelation that I am so excited about and now you are telling me not to respond when my big red button is pushed?"

She wasn't sure how that could be possible, but over the years, as she applied the knowledge of the love of God in her life, little by little the many cords and wires connected to her red button were clipped, and she was successful in disengaging the "big red nasty" as she calls it.

Tamy got her revelation of the big red button, but I received an illustration of how offense worked in my life in a little different way. I too was convinced that my husband was the source of offense in our marriage. He had several precise ways he could upset me because, well, Brad inherited his love language from me. Words or tone of voice that I perceived to be unkind or insensitive hurt like crazy, and it wasn't easy to get over either.

I tried for years to convey to my husband that if he wouldn't speak to me in an offensive way, then I wouldn't get offended. For some reason, he never seemed to comprehend the term "offensive." To him, he was just saying what he thought. I had tried every way I knew to get him to change. Finally, one day, the Lord showed me a lamp with a big red bulb in it. A chain was hanging from the lamp to turn it on. Then I watched an evil little imp sneak up to the light and jerk the string. Of course, the glaring red light came on. After that, I heard the Spirit of God say, "If you can be offended, you will get offended."

I thought, *Is it possible to get to the place where you can't be offended, no matter how you are treated?*

That was a new thought. Then, God revealed to me that there are spirits of offense commissioned to do nothing else except pull the chains of unsuspecting individuals to whom they are assigned. I figured that if I insisted on keeping the bulb of offense in my life, each and every time my chain was pulled, my red light would come on without fail. It just stood to reason the only way I could keep from getting offended was to change bulbs.

The only way that could happen was to install the brilliant flood light of love in my light socket instead of the angry red bulb of offense. As a result, when that nasty spirit of offense slithered around to yank my chain, he would be blinded by forgiveness. As a result, the light of Jesus Christ would shine out of my life instead of anger, resentment, and hurt. I could just visualize the devil shaking his fist and shouting, "Curses! Foiled again!"

When I saw that, I determined to get rid of a spirit of offense. I commanded him to get out of my life and out of my marriage, and thankfully, our relationship has never been the same. I was delighted to find things that used to offend me didn't have the same effect they used to. Can I say I have never been tempted to get offended again? No, no, of course not, and I can't boast that I have never yielded to that spirit of offense. But, when I do, I know it and start the process of kicking him out once again.

7

The Other Side of the Coin

Mahatma Gandhi made the statement: "The weak can never forgive. Forgiveness is the attribute of the strong." La Rochefoucauld said, "Only the brave know how to forgive. One pardons in the degree that one loves." Walking in love is not for wimps. It takes a person who is strong in character to love and forgive like God does.

Love is like a coin with two sides: giving and forgiving. You can't foster a loving relationship without being skilled in the practice of forgiveness. Forgiveness is the main ingredient in the bloodline of a Christian. It allows all the functions of the body of Christ to work together in a healthy, peaceful manner, permitting it to grow to full stature and maturity. Unforgiveness is like cholesterol in the spiritual blood veins of a believer. It hardens the arteries and leads to heart problems, stifling spiritual growth and produces division and a strife-filled environment.

Therapist Beverly Flanigan, a clinical professor of social work at the University of Wisconsin, says, "Forgiveness is a powerful tool. Whether you have been abused by a parent, dumped by a spouse, abandoned by a child, or betrayed by a friend, forgiveness is a process that allows you to reframe even the most hurtful injury, reframe how you regard the person who hurt you, ditch the anger and hatred that seals you in a negative force field, and allows you to move on with your life.

"It's one of the few means you have to free yourself of the past. There just aren't that many profound psychological processes that will give you the opportunity to start again. You can change where you live, you can change jobs, but to change yourself—to transform your damaged psyche and soul after the devastation of betrayal, injury, or the abandonment of an intimate connection—and start over with a different view of life, this is one of the few avenues available.

"Studies show that the anger left behind in the wake of devastating injuries like abuse, abandonment, and betrayal alter your emotional landscape so drastically that forever after you see the world through a filter of negativity that leaves you feeling anxious, distrustful, and depressed. And because these negative feelings stimulate a cascade of hormones that accelerate your heart rate, shut down your immune system, and encourage blood clotting, not only do you often find happiness illusive, but you're also at increased risk of heart attack, stroke, high blood pressure, cancer, and a slew of other chronic illnesses. So forgiveness isn't just 'nice' to do, researchers agree, it is essential to a happy, healthy life."

The Bitter Skunk Syndrome

The Apostle Paul agrees with this clinical study because he advises in Ephesians 4: 31–32:

> Let all bitterness and indignation and wrath (passion, rage, bad temper) and resentment (anger, animosity) and quarreling (brawling, clamor, contention) and slander (evil-speaking, abusive or blas-

phemous language) be banished from you, with all
malice (spite, ill will, or baseness of any kind).

And become useful and helpful and kind to
one another, tenderhearted (compassionate, understanding, loving hearted), forgiving one another
[readily and freely], as God in Christ forgave you.

Those descriptive words from the preceding scripture
paint a vivid picture of someone who has held unforgiveness in his heart until it has turned into the contaminating
poison of bitterness. The words Paul uses, like wrath, contention, anger, and ill will, and so on, are the fruit that grow
when you don't forgive.

In stark contrast, Paul describes what happens to the
behavior of someone who makes the decision to forgive.
Those who forgive are not only people who have become
useful, helpful, and kind but individuals who are tenderhearted, compassionate, and loving hearted as well. Which
of those two groups would you like to be in a relationship with? If you say, "The kind, tenderhearted person, of
course." Then that's what you must be if you want others to
enjoy being around you.

When bitterness sends down its roots into the heart of
anyone who has been hurt or mistreated, every relationship
surrounding that offended person is in trouble.

Hebrews 12:15 reveals how important it is to learn how
to obtain the grace of God enabling you to forgive, "in order
that no root of resentment (rancor, bitterness, or hatred)
shoots forth and causes trouble and bitter torment, and the
many become contaminated and defiled by it."

The writer of Hebrews warns that bitterness retained in
your heart will, first of all, torment you, and then eventually, contaminate and defile any one you are around for very

long. It will pollute your life much like a skunk infects the very atmosphere he inhabits when he is riled.

We came home one evening after dark from a dinner meeting when I remembered I hadn't fed the cats. We feed them in an enclosed gazebo out back. I hurriedly grabbed a can of cat food, and just as I was bending over to empty it into their bowl, I saw a movement in the shadowy corner to my left. When my eyes adjusted to the darkness, I detected a huge, black tail all fanned out with the business end aimed at me hooked to a suspicious looking animal with a white stripe down his back. I ran faster than a speeding bullet getting out of that gazebo and into the house. In a split second, I was out of range. I believe it is a good defensive maneuver to leave quickly when a skunk is in your vicinity.

If you really look at a skunk, they are pretty cute animals, but they seem to have trouble sustaining close relationships. It's all because of their *stinking* attitude.

There are people like that who have developed stinking, rotten attitudes because they have allowed a root of bitterness to overrun their lives. When you don't deal with resentment, you become a bitter person, and no one wants to stay around you for very long—any more than I wanted to take a chance with the skunk I encountered in the gazebo.

Most bitter people will swear they are not bitter. They are blind to how their behavior affects others and have determined, "That's just the way I am." To expose some long-standing deception for those who are unaware of their hazardous attitude, here is a picture of a bitter person:

A person who is bitter...
is hostile and has a sharp tongue;
is touchy and easily offended;

is picky and critical;
is self-centered;
is insensitive;
has hardness of heart;
is demanding;
is quick to withdraw;
has a revengeful spirit;
is ill-tempered;
has ill will;
is moody;
is preoccupied with the past;
is suspicious and distrustful;
consistently projects wrong motives on others;
is unable to respond to affection or give genuine affection to others;
is unable to communicate without hostility.

Bitterness is painful to live around. The only way to untangle its mess in a person's heart is to genuinely forgive.

How to Forgive

The main question is "how can I forgive the person who has viciously hurt and betrayed me, when all I feel is resentment, and bitterness?" I struggled with that question for years because of my tendency to be overly sensitive, probably due to my melancholy temperament. Every perceived offense drove a knife into my gut so deep that I couldn't have hurt more if I had literally been struck in the stomach with a ball bat. It took days, and sometimes even weeks or years, before I could feel even slightly normal. As a result, I kept a protective wall around my feelings, refusing to allow myself to trust anyone. Therefore, I was not able to freely give or properly receive affection. That's a miserable kind of existence. It cuts you off from enjoying any relationship to its fullest.

I knew God had to have the answer because he is an expert at forgiving even the vilest sinner, so I cried out to him to help me forgive more easily. I learned how to forgive when the Holy Spirit drew my attention to Ephesians 4:2 from the Amplified Bible, giving me an all-important key:

"Living as becomes you with complete lowliness of mind (humility) and meekness (unselfishness, gentleness, mildness), with patience, bearing with one another and *making allowances because you love one another*." (emphasis mine)

That term "making allowances" jumped out at me. As I meditated on what it meant to make allowances, a picture emerged in my mind. I saw myself approach the front door of a building intending to go outside; but there, positioned just outside the entrance, was a huge dog staring at me with a fierce, menacing look. His lips were curled into a vicious snarl. Saliva dripped from long fangs that were bared as he growled in a threatening way.

When I saw that terrifying picture, naturally I was frightened and wanted to call someone to come and kill that crazy dog, but then I took a second look. I saw that the dog's hind leg was partially severed, hanging by a thin piece of skin and a few tendons, with bones protruding. Blood gushed profusely from the wound. Upon seeing that, my focus changed. I quit looking at the *behavior* of the dog and started to pay attention to his *need*. Right away, the fear and hostility toward the dog drained away, and in its place, compassion welled up. I then wanted to call someone that could help the dog instead of kill him. As I watched that incident in my mind's eye, I knew I was seeing what

Paul meant when he encouraged us to "make allowances" because we love one another.

The Spirit of God said to me: "If the wounds people have were on the outside instead of the inside, you would have more compassion for them."

It is true; people who are hurting have a tendency to hurt others. I discovered that forgiveness is much easier if I focus on the *needs* in the lives of those who mistreat me instead of paying so much attention to their *behavior*.

One of the most vital steps to forgive successfully is to develop the habit of making allowances for those who wrong you, just like Jesus did when he was cruelly and unjustly beaten. As he looked at his executioners from the agony of the cross, he cried, "Father, forgive them for they know not what they do!"

Instead of demanding vengeance for those who heartlessly mistreated him—and he could have called ten thousand warring angels that would have turned his persecutors into toast—he made allowances and forgave them. Consequently, he died free from the inner pain produced by not forgiving, and he offers that same forgiveness to us as well.

Forgiving the Unforgivable

A thirty-two-year-old woman named Carol entered the hospital room where her mother lay dying from a stroke and brain cancer. As she looked at the pitiful sight of the frail and twisted form lying on the bed before her, she hardly knew what to do. Even though the pathetic woman struggled to speak and feebly extended her hand, Carol hesitated to respond.

What am I supposed to do? She thought. *Play the dutiful daughter? Love a woman who had never for one single second of one single minute of one single day ever showed that she loved me?*

Carol and her mother had never been close. In fact, their relationship was one filled with bitterness and abuse. Carol understood from the time she was little that her mom had problems. She could remember visiting her in the hospital where she would be zoned out on shock treatments. Her mother would then come home and be a zombie. Finally, when the treatments wore off, she'd be back to her normal self.

Her mother's normal self was horrific. She would waken Carol at two in the morning and rip into her legs with coat hangers for no reason. Carol had to go to school with all the wounds showing.

Carol loved school. It was the one safe place where she could melt into the crowd and forget about her crazy mother at home. She loved to learn and loved to write. In fact, because of her writing, she was offered the opportunity to attend a four-year college and get a degree in journalism from New Jersey's *Courier Post* newspaper, which would sponsor her tuition. All she had to do was stay in school and graduate. It was like a dream come true. However, on Carol's sixteenth birthday, her mother dragged her out of bed, slapped her in the face, and said that today was the day she had to quit school and take charge of her three younger siblings full-time.

Crying and sobbing, she was marched into her principal's office. Even her teachers were crying as her mother signed her out, and there went her dream.

Even though Carol was devastated, she did what her mother told her and spent the next year taking care of her brothers and sisters and working part-time. Then, just after her seventeenth birthday, her mother threw her out.

She came home from work and found that her mother had thrown her clothes out the window. They were littering the street, and she was screaming out the window that now that her baby sister was getting older, she didn't need her. She could just hit the road.

Carol moved into a boardinghouse and worked at retail jobs, dividing most of her paycheck between her father who had left home and her mother.

Eventually, Carol earned her GED, took a few college courses, married and divorced, married and was widowed, married and is still married to a wonderful man with whom she has raised six incredible children—two of hers, three of his, and one of theirs.

During those years, Carol had always made time to do her mother's grocery shopping, hang her wash, or stop by her house and cook her something to eat.

Carol never abandoned the woman who abandoned her. In Carol's case, her amazing capacity for empathy and understanding may have provided the key to restoration. Even when her mother was ripping into her legs, she could see the pain that her mother was in. She couldn't explain it, but she knew and felt and understood that if her mother hadn't been ill, she would have been able to show love instead of anger. So instead of Carol seeing a monster coming at her, sometimes, she would close her eyes and imagine a mother of seven who was normal, who would come home from work and gather up the clothes and do the normal things that mothers do.

As Longfellow once wrote, "If we could read the secret history of our enemies, we should find in each man's life sorrow and suffering enough to disarm all hostility."

So standing that day in her mother's hospital room, as the woman reached toward her, Carol prayed, "Oh God, tell me what to do."

In her mind, Carol heard the still small voice of the Lord saying, "Comfort her. Love her. Love her as you wanted to be loved when you were a child."

Slowly, tears started down Carol's cheeks. Then she did what she had done with her own daughter when she had awakened from a bad dream—she got into bed with her mother. Gently, she gathered her mother into her arms. Her mother groaned; and Carol held her tighter, crooning to her, telling her not to be afraid, that she was there, and that she would stay with her. Filled with pity and compassion, she stroked her mother's hair and whispered into her ear that she loved her, and that she had always loved her.

Her mother's slight figure relaxed in Carol's arms and her breathing changed. Carol knew her mother was nearing the end of her struggle.

"Forgive her. And then tell her about me," she heard God whisper.

Peace filled Carol; and she knew this was something she needed to do, not only for her mother but also for herself. The monster had ceased to exist. In her arms was only a woman in pain and fear.

Carol told her that she forgave her, completely, while her tears fell in her mother's hair. Then she told her about God, a God of unconditional love, of everlasting love. She told her how to receive peace from God and assured her that he was waiting to receive her spirit.

When Carol looked into her mother's face, the fear had left. Then her mother smiled. The smile was so beautiful, so filled with love as innocent and pure as Carol's children's smiles. Then with a sigh as gentle and as quiet as that of a contented child, she died.

Gently God whispered again, "Forgive her?"

And Carol whispered, "Yes God, I have."

Carol was a woman who had learned how to make allowances and as a result was able to forgive her mother completely. Because of her choice to forgive, Carol lived out the rest of her life free from the misery of bitterness and the pain of the past.

Vengeance Belongs to God

Since we are all imperfect humans, what are we going to do with other people's sins, imperfections, inconsistencies, or immaturities? The human tendency is to develop a plan of vengeance when someone hurts you. Evil for evil; insult for insult; you did it to me, so I'll do it back to you because you deserve it.

Many times, we are prone to think like our daughter Kim did when she and Brad were young during their sibling rivalry stage. One day, I caught them hitting each other, so I called a truce. When I tried to get to the bottom of the conflict, Kim piped up offering an explanation. Pointing an accusing finger at Brad, she stated adamantly, "He started it." I thought this would be an opportune time to teach her the golden rule, so I recited Luke 6:31 about "doing unto others as you would have them do to you."

"Well Mom," she retorted, "that's what I was doing. He did it to me, so I was just doing it back to him."

I explained to her several times that the golden rule says you do unto others only what you want them to do back to you. Each time I got the same reply. "I know Mom. He did it to me, so I did it back to him." I finally got frustrated because I felt she was just not getting it. For some reason, she thought I was not getting it either. Finally, I gave up and closed the book on that lesson for the time being. When she got older, she was able to explain her thinking about that incident. She pointed out that what she was doing was trying to teach Brad the golden rule. Since he was hitting her, that's what he wanted her to do back to him. She was giving him his harvest from the seeds he planted in her life.

But Paul told the Romans in chapter twelve, verses 17–21:

> Repay no one evil for evil, but take thought for what is honest and proper and noble [aiming to be above reproach] in the sight of everyone. If possible, as far as it depends on you, live at peace with everyone.
>
> Beloved, never avenge yourselves, but leave the way open for [God's] wrath; for it is written, Vengeance is Mine, I will repay (requite), says the Lord. But if your enemy is hungry, feed him; if he is thirsty, give him drink; for by so doing you will heap burning coals upon his head. Do not let yourself be overcome by evil, but overcome (master) evil with good.

Paul clarified the harvest question. If someone acts mean, they definitely have a harvest coming, but who is responsible to give them their harvest? Does the person who is being mistreated have a right to return to the offender the harvest due him—like Kim was doing to Brad? Paul answered that question: If evil has been done to you, it is not your place to give the person who injured you his harvest. Instead, vengeance belongs to God and he will repay. God is the only one who is qualified to bring about the harvest.

When someone offends, they are planting hurtful seeds, and when harvested, the results will have a disastrous effect on their lives. But often, we have a tendency to take those same damaging seeds that others have planted in our lives and in return, sow them back in the offender's life, creating a destructive harvest cycle that will ultimately come back to us as well.

If you don't want a sandbur crop, don't plant stickers. Have you ever been walking around outside in the fall of the year and accidentally stepped on a sticker? The first thing you probably did was jerk it out. You didn't leave it in your body and go around crying about it or call someone on the phone and have them pray with you. I doubt that you carried it around still stuck in your hand or foot for days, weeks, or even years, showing it to everyone you met in order to get sympathy. No. You got it out immediately, babied the spot for just a few minutes, and then forgot about it.

I know you didn't go out and plant the stupid seed so you would have more sandburs, but that's what many people do when someone offends them. They hug the offense until it festers and becomes inflamed. Then, they show off their horrible injury to everyone they meet, waiting for that pitiful pat on the back that assures them they have been terribly victimized.

The most destructive thing they can do is find a handy little sandbur of their own and plant it back in the life of the one who hurt them. If you do that, then a crop of sandburs will grow up, and you will reap an abundant harvest of pain and misery. Then, the vicious cycle continues—sandbur for sandbur, sticker for sticker until both individuals reap a harvest of destruction.

When someone plants a sandbur of offense in you, it would be in your best interest to sow some *other* kind of seed so you won't get the same harvest they are going to get. The best thing you can do in such a situation is get off the merry-go-round and do something different.

Paul makes a suggestion. Find a flower seed to plant or some other kind of seed that will produce a pleasant harvest. Don't plant the same kind of seed the offender has planted if you don't want his harvest. He says it this way: Do something good for your enemy. When you do, you can successfully overcome any evil from that circumstance and experience something beneficial instead.

Paul also points out that when you do good, you leave the way open for God's wrath. When someone hurts you, the thought of God's wrath coming upon them just doesn't seem all that bad. Actually, it probably seems like an extremely good idea, the more wrath the better, in fact. A few scorching, sizzling, searing coals of really blistering quality piled on the offender's head would be a terrific suggestion. However, God's wrath doesn't mean he will send fire down from heaven and zap the offender, even though sometimes we wish that's the way he would handle it. No, the meaning of God's wrath is his hand extended into a situation to bring justice. Now isn't that what we really wanted all along?

If you will cooperate with God and let him bring the harvest—because the Bible says he is the "Lord of the harvest"—and plant those life-giving seeds of love and forgiveness, he can then take an offense, which was designed to trap you and control your life with its negative poison, and bring only good out of it for you.

What are the best seeds to plant in the lives of the people who have wronged you? The apostle Peter described them in 1 Peter 3: 9–11:

> Never return evil for evil or insult for insult (scolding, tongue-lashing, berating), but on the contrary blessing [praying for their welfare, happiness, and protection, and truly pitying and loving them]. For know that to this you have been called, that you may yourselves inherit a blessing [from God—that you may obtain a blessing as heirs, bringing welfare and happiness and protection].
>
> For let him who wants to enjoy life and see good days [good—whether apparent or not] keep his tongue free from evil and his lips from guile (treachery, deceit).
>
> Let him turn away from wickedness and shun it, and let him do right. Let him search for peace (harmony; undisturbedness from fears, agitating passions, and moral conflicts) and seek it eagerly. [Do not merely desire peaceful relations with God, with your fellowmen, and with yourself, but pursue, go after them!].

When life hands you sandburs, trash them. Grab the seeds that Peter talked about and plant blessings instead. Pray for welfare, happiness, and protection for those who have been malicious toward you, and as a result, you will qualify to inherit a harvest of blessing enjoying life and experiencing good days. When you forgive an offense and plant good seeds, it doesn't nullify the wrong they have done; it nullifies its negative effect in your life.

Self-inflicted Wounds

Byron Katie was a woman with three children. After she experienced a painful divorce, she became a woman full of rage, paranoia, with suicidal depression, and morbidly obese. Secluded in the attic of a halfway house for troubled women, she had a revelation that changed her life. Part of that revelation included "suffering over things that have happened to you is nothing more than an argument with the past. Your Father may have slapped you when you were three, but now you have done it a million times to yourself by replaying the incident over and over. On your deathbed, you can still be saying he or she ruined my life. Forgiving those who hurt you and retiring the stressful thoughts associated with those incidents could be the most important retirement there is. Reality is always much kinder than our thoughts about it!"

When you experience a special event in your life, often you record it as a video on your cell phone or make a DVD so you can watch it over and over. The devil does the same thing. Every time someone offends you, he records that event then hands you the movie so you can watch it day and night should you desire to do so. He wants that to become you favorite pastime. When the offense starts to fade in your memory, Satan's plan is that you drag out the video and watch it play out in all the drama you can muster in your imagination. Consequently, every emotion you felt during the initial injury reoccurs with vengeance. I call that self-inflicted wounds. It's not the offense that hurts you at that point. Now you are hurting yourself.

Emotions are created by what you think and say. They can be created at any time, and they can be changed at will. One of my husband's favorite movies is *Where the Red Fern*

Grows because his number one hobby is 'coon hunting. Every time we watch that movie, it goes without saying we have to plop down a box of Kleenex between us because we know at the end the tears will flow. We both know that Little Ann and Old Dan are just dogs that know how to act and they don't really die, but it sure seems real to us. So those sad emotions are created, and we both sit there bawling.

That's what happens with our videos of offense. We always know how it's going to end: we are the victim, and we have been wronged. Therefore, every emotion we originally felt is recreated, and the cycle of not forgiving goes on and on until our emotions are so warped we don't know reality from fantasy.

The only way you can truly forgive is to choose to destroy the video. The meaning of the word forgiveness is "aphieimi," which means "to send off, to release, to let go of or let be, to hurl away as with a missile."

To have the ability to forgive, you can't afford to rehearse the offense over and over. You must fling it away just like you would a venomous snake tormenting you with his poison. You can't play with rattlesnakes and not expect to get bitten, nor can you be entertained with the video of how "they did me wrong" and not have tumultuous emotions either.

When you pray blessings on those who hurt you, it changes the video. Your emotions change, and you quit being the victim. Instead, you become the conquering hero who overcomes by doing the right thing—so the story ends in victory instead of defeat.

Free at Last

The 700 Club aired in April 2006 a testimony of Gilbert, a young man who had a lot of offense directed his way. The offense that threatened to destroy him did not defeat him in the end because he learned how to handle it effectively.

Gilbert's father was a very violent man and occasionally threatened Gilbert with a gun. Gilbert had just turned fourteen when he started daydreaming about wrestling the gun away from his dad and shooting him. He thought that was the only way to stop his father from killing him or anyone else in the house. Consumed and tortured by this thought, he prayed to the God of his maternal grandmother. "If you are as powerful as Granny says, God, why don't you do something?"

Not long afterward, someone invited him to church. To his surprise, his father did not stop him from going. At church, the minister talked about God's love and quoted John 3:16: "For God so loved the world that he gave his one and only son, that whoever believes in him shall not perish but have eternal life."

"The best part of all," the minister explained, "is that it doesn't matter that you feel undeserving. God's love and forgiveness are gifts."

Gilbert knew a lot about feeling undeserving, unforgiven, and guilty; his dad had made sure of that. He felt like everything terrible his father did was his fault. This new promise he heard was his only hope. As he prayed, God's love filled him. That prayer seemed to change everything.

After that, he continued to pray and study the Bible he had been given. It taught him to pray for those who hurt him, including his dad. It taught him that he should love God, serve him, and fear no man. At church, a teacher who was open and honest about spiritual things said, "Life isn't going to be perfect just because we are Christians. We still have to live in a sin-polluted world like everyone else."

When he returned home from church one evening, he found his Dad beating his Mom with a gun. Without thinking, he forced himself between them.

Suddenly, Gilbert felt the cold, steel muzzle of his father's gun pressed against his temple. "One of these days I am going to blow your head off," his father said in a calculated, convincing tone, "I'm sick and tired of your interfering."

Gilbert should have been terrified, but he felt a supernatural peace. No longer did he have the desire to kill his father as he had before. During those past four years, something had changed.

Here, he was about to turn eighteen with his earthly father shoving a gun to his head. He knew he had to trust his Heavenly Father with his life. What could he say that would make a difference? Suddenly, he recalled God's words: "Do not fear, for I am with you…I will strengthen you and help you."

He raised his head and stared into his father's eyes. In a steady but soft voice he said, "If that's what you want to do, Dad, go ahead and pull the trigger. I'm ready to die. I know I will go to heaven where you can't hurt me anymore. But remember this: someday you will stand before God and be held accountable for your actions." There was no fear in Gilbert's eyes, but for the first time, he saw a hint of fear in his father's. His father never threatened him that way again.

A year later, he, his mom, his brother and sister fled from Texas to California to get away from his dad, but he found them anyway. His father begged them to come back, swearing he had changed. During Christmas vacation, his dad came and got them. However, Gilbert had a job that he liked. He knew he could never live with his father again, so he did not go.

Several nights later, Gilbert got a phone call telling him that his mother was in the hospital and not expected to live. While his brother and sister lay sleeping in their rooms at the back of the house, his dad had beaten his mother in the head with a hammer and left her for dead. The police found and arrested his father the next morning.

Gilbert's mother survived, but it was over a month before she was well enough to leave the hospital. His dad pleaded temporary insanity at his trial. Like salt in a wound, the defense falsely accused him and his mother of being prostitutes to better his father's case. His anger and bitterness increased with each lie his father spoke during his testimony. Even though he prayed over and over for God to help them, when the verdict was pronounced, his dad was found guilty of premeditated attempted murder and was sentenced to only three and a half years in prison.

After the trial, Gilbert and his siblings moved away. They were finally free, except Gilbert had become a prisoner—a prisoner of bitterness. He loved God. He knew no rational person could blame God for the evil choices people made, but that knowledge did not stop his all-consuming hatred for his dad. As the hate festered, it took all the joy out of his life. As he turned twenty, he couldn't understand why he felt so old and lifeless. God's word nudged him toward forgiveness, but he refused.

"Dad doesn't deserve forgiveness!" he argued. Then, God reminded him through his word that Gilbert hadn't deserved forgiveness either. Even if he had wanted to forgive his dad, he felt it was humanly impossible to do so. But then he reasoned, if God had helped him have no fear that time his dad had pressed the gun to his head—and that had certainly seemed humanly impossible—then surely he could help him forgive. He wanted with all his heart to obey God, yet he couldn't imagine forgiving the man who had brutalized his family. He knew God would never force him to do anything against his will, so he prayed, "Help me, Lord, to want to forgive my dad."

A few months later, a powerful desire to choose to forgive his father suddenly enveloped him. His tears washed away the last remnant of resentment as he whispered into an empty room, "I forgive you, Dad, for everything."

At last he was free. Forever!

Gilbert discovered what we all should know: God's commandments are not given to make our lives miserable. When he demands that we do something that seems hard, it is always for our good.

"For the [true] love of God is this: that we do His commands [keep His ordinances and are mindful of His precepts and teaching]. And these orders of His are not irksome (burdensome, oppressive, or grievous)" (1 John. 5:3).

One of the most important decisions you can make, if you want to enjoy great relationships, is to refuse to be offended by anyone or at anything. No matter how you are treated or what anyone says to you, determine to quickly forgive and let it drop. Resist the temptation to entertain the offense in your thoughts, words, or actions. If you do this, you will have dismantled the devil's most powerful trap. You can trip his trap before he can trip you up!

This is word the Lord spoke to me about handling offense:

"It's not what others do to you that matters in your life. It's what you do, with what they've done, that determines peace or strife. You always have a choice to make when facing every test. So, child, when you choose my way, you've chosen to be blessed!"

8

Stop Allowing Yourself to Get Aggravated

I groaned as I reluctantly hauled my protesting body out of bed. Wouldn't you know it, I had overslept. Of all mornings, this was one day when I should have popped right out of bed at the crack of dawn.

It was the summer of 1966 and my husband and I, along with our twenty-one-month-old son, Quentin, had just moved to the Panhandle of Texas where Charlie had taken the job of managing a nineteen-section ranch. Part of the benefits of the job was the privilege of living in a large, sprawling two-story house that could have been quite elegant and probably had been in its prime. Even though it was an older house, it still had a lot of class. There were beautiful hardwood floors in the entryway and living areas, high ceilings, and a veranda that ran around the front and side. It seemed like a mansion to me because before, we had lived in a small trailer house.

But now, I had thirteen large rooms, three bathrooms, a huge kitchen, and hardly any furniture. I loved all the space, but with a busy toddler, it was difficult to keep up with all the cleaning it required. Most of the time, I'll have to admit it had that lived-in look—except when we were going to have company. When expecting visitors, I wanted everything to look just right, so I spent extra time mopping and waxing the wood floors and meticulously dusting and vacuuming.

That particular morning, I surveyed the room in dismay remembering Charlie's brother and his wife were coming to visit the ranch for the first time that evening. Everywhere I looked, I saw only disarray. Piles of dirty clothes leered at me from every corner of the room, silently challenging my courage and determination. They were strewn about exactly where we had tossed them the night before when we dragged in weary and tired from spending the weekend with Charlie's parents.

I yawned as I glanced at the clock. Getting everything done was going to be a race against time. Hurriedly, I threw on some work clothes, suppressing the gnawing anxiety already churning down on the inside. Quickly, I checked on Quentin. If only he would sleep late, then I could get started on the mopping and waxing. No such luck.

With one eye on the clock, I hurried Quentin through his breakfast, and with a sigh of relief, watched him scurry out the front door to find Daddy down at the barn. Good. Now I could concentrate on scrubbing and waxing those hardwood floors I was so proud of. Just as I wrung out my mop for the last time, the faucet made a sickening gurgle.

"Oh no," I gasped, "please, not today." Frantically, I twisted both handles on the faucet. My heart sank. Where there had been a steady flow of water before, now only a few drops remained. Those too diminished and soon disappeared before my panic-stricken eyes. "Of all days to run out of water," I wailed, "this can't be happening."

We had a windmill that provided water to both the stock tanks and the storage unit that fed water to the house.

Periodically, the supply had to be switched back and forth to keep both tanks full. Charlie had forgotten to make the switch from the stock tanks to the house storage tank, so until the wind blew enough to run the windmill, we were out of water in the house.

Already, I felt aggravation stirring on the inside. I rubbed my temples, trying to suppress the first twinges of a headache. Now what was I going to do? The morning was practically gone, and I had only just begun to clean. There was washing yet to be done, dusting to do, floors to vacuum, beds to change, and lunch to fix. The elaborate evening meal I had planned for my company still lay neatly wrapped, tucked away in the refrigerator. The clock taunted me from the kitchen wall, gleefully ticking away precious minutes.

Suddenly, I heard a frantic scream come from the direction of the garden. Alarmed, I rushed outside and found Quentin clutching his leg as he leaned against the trash barrel. When I surveyed the injured area, I found a deep cut bleeding profusely. After investigating, I discovered the source of the injury was a broken fruit jar. I wiped away the tears from Quentin's eyes while tears of exasperation welled up in mine. After cleaning the cut the best I could without water, I stomped off to find Charlie, complaining and muttering to myself the whole way.

He was in the barn, doctoring his favorite horse that had just got bitten by a rattlesnake. I proceeded to vent the anger and frustration on Charlie that had been building all morning as though he was the cause of the aggravation. He agreed to drive Quentin twenty miles to town to have the cut treated and get a tetanus shot. Then to pacify me, he promised to get a water truck to haul some water.

I was partially relieved though still shaking with anger. Once again, I plunged into cleaning the house. As I finished dusting, I nervously surveyed the living room. Not bad! The floors gleamed, highlighting the natural beauty of the wood grain. Aware of the ominous ticking of the clock, I hastily picked up an ivy plant to return it to its place of prominence on the now-lustrous coffee table. Because I was in such a hurry, I neglected to get a firm grip on the pot, and as I turned, it slipped from my fingers and went sailing all over my freshly waxed floor. Potting soil clung wildly to the just-vacuumed rug positioned in the center of the room, and my once gleaming floor was now splattered with dirt and mud.

I screamed out to the empty room, "I have had it! I can't take anymore."

You've heard of the straw that broke the camel's back, well, that was it. I bolted out the front door sobbing, totally overwhelmed. My husband, who had just returned with Quentin, heard all the noise and came running, expecting to find that some horrible disaster had happened. Through uncontrollable tears, I angrily told him about my latest mishap and then jumped in the car and ran away from home. It was only for an hour or so, but to say I was a basket case was an understatement.

When I finally returned in a somewhat calmer state of mind, Charlie had cleaned up the mess in my absence. Everything looked great again. Later on that evening, our unsuspecting company arrived to a very clean house that looked normal and peaceful, never realizing the drama that had transpired that day.

You are probably thinking, "What was the big deal with the broken plant? Just go with the flow, roll with the punches, keep a stiff upper lip, and pull yourself up by the boot straps. Things happen, and we just have to deal with it." Well that's easy for you to say, but in those days, it certainly wasn't easy for me to do. In fact, I have to admit I was easily upset. And, things that are not balanced very well will get upset easily!

There was an imbalance in my life back then that I had not identified. Now, I have come to realize the main reason a person gets aggravated easily is because he or she needs to be in control. When we're inconvenienced by circumstances, or when things do not go as we would like, we feel we have a right to get upset. And when someone does not act or do what we think they should, it aggravates us. So we live our lives thinking circumstances or imperfect people are the problem, convinced that we have to get aggravated if they don't line up with what we think should be done.

Jesus didn't think that way. He addressed the problem in John 14:27:

> Peace I leave with you; My [own] peace I now give and bequeath to you. Not as the world gives do I give to you. *Do not let your hearts be troubled, neither let them be afraid. [Stop allowing yourselves to be agitated and disturbed;* and do not permit yourselves to be fearful and intimidated and cowardly and unsettled]. (emphasis mine)

Notice that Jesus said, "Do not let, and stop allowing yourself to be agitated and disturbed." When we go around saying, "Oh that just aggravates me," or "They make me so aggravated," or even, "If such and such happens, I'm going to get aggravated," we don't just allow ourselves to get agitated, we precondition ourselves to become aggravated.

To be accurate, we should say, I *let* that circumstance make me aggravated, or I *allowed* myself to get aggravated at that person. You permit aggravation in your life because you choose to. No person or circumstance can steal your peace unless you let them. In any given situation, you have two choices: to get aggravated or to maintain your peace. It's your choice; and whether it seems like it or not, it is a choice!

Many people can't cope with the everyday pressures that arise and are thrown into a state of "temporary insanity" by unexpected predicaments like I was on that fateful day at the ranch. Even slight variations make them agitated and angry, blowing the whole situation out of proportion.

Let's face it: life is not always like a memory foam mattress. Husbands, wives, children, friends, or even mothers-in-law may not always say or do what we think they should. Circumstances will seldom be completely in our favor, but we have an option about how we react.

Maintaining Peace

In relationships, if one or both persons insist on getting aggravated every time there is a glitch in the plan of things, that relationship is in danger of being in a constant state of upheaval. To create and maintain relationships that are healthy and stable, the subject of aggravation has to be addressed.

Aggravate means "to provoke or exasperate; arouse to anger; to make worse; to intensify as in an offense." A companion word, *agitate*, is close in meaning, described as "keeping a subject or cause under continuous discussion, and creating strong or tumultuous emotions."

Those definitions remind me of the washing machine my mother used when I was a child. Monday was wash day at our house. I remember waking up to the rhythmic, pulsating sound of the motor attached to our antiquated washing machine. Even though it was old-fashioned, my dad had rigged it with electricity. Mounted on the top was a wringer with two black rubber cylinders through which the dripping clothes were carefully guided, piece by piece, until the water-soaked laundry was squeezed into a state of mere dampness. My mom threw the dirty garments into a big open tub where, for a full quarter of an hour, they endured a severe beating from a device positioned in the center of the tub called an agitator. For at least fifteen minutes, the agitator constantly stirred the clothes, pounding the dirt in them out into the wash water.

Aggravation works the same way. Every bit of hidden dirt is squeezed into your thought life when you allow yourself to get agitated until strong tumultuous emotions of fear or anger are created from every nasty situation whether the source is circumstances or people.

One of the most important lessons you can learn is how to maintain peace on the inside when the storms of life buffet you from the outside. With peace at the helm, instead of getting aggravated, you can simply allow your inner calmness to still the storm. That's what Jesus did in Mark 4:35–41. When he and his disciples were crossing to the other side of the lake, there arose without warning a furious storm of hurricane proportions. The waves beat against the boat so violently that the boat began to fill with water and started to sink.

The disciples woke Jesus who was asleep in the stern of the boat as they cried out, "Master, do you not care that we are perishing?"

Jesus stretched, rubbed his eyes for a moment, assessed the turbulent waves, then with confident composure arose and rebuked the wind. "Hush now! Be still and muzzled!" The wind ceased immediately and a great calm and perfect peacefulness prevailed.

When the disciples stood awestruck at the unusual turn of events, Jesus then confronted them about their serious issues with faith and trust. Because the disciples were in turmoil on the inside and filled with fear, the storm had threatened to overwhelm them. The disciples could not affect the tempest with peace because they had none. They had been in a state of serious agitation, but Jesus, on the other hand, had perfect peace; after all, he had planned to sleep through the storm until being so rudely awakened.

The ability to maintain peace in your life hinges on faith and trust. If you insist on being in control, that's where your faith and trust will be. You must depend on your own power, with the responsibility of getting everything fixed in your world resting on your shoulders. That scenario presents a disaster ready to happen because your ability to be God is greatly limited. You can fix a few things with your intellect and wisdom, but a great many problems are beyond your control.

If you want to maintain peace, you must realize that circumstances beyond your control *are* beyond your control! If you could have brought about a change, you would have already done it. In order to see some significant difference, it can't be your problem anymore. At some point, you have to trust God with the outcome.

When you are *not* trusting God, even slight annoyances will cause you to grumble and complain. Continued aggravation produces anger, dissatisfaction, vexation, and most of all, worry; all of which greatly disturbs, first of all your peace, and then secondly, wreaks havoc in any relationship.

The children of Israel were prime examples of how *not* to handle adverse situations. Immediately after God gloriously delivered them from Egypt, they ran out of food, there was no water to be found, and they were getting a little aggravated because Moses was always running the show.

Everything they were not satisfied with caused them to murmur and complain. However, time after time, God supernaturally intervened in spite of their rotten attitudes.

When they finally approached the banks of the Jordan, even though they had complained all the way, they arrived well-fed, well watered, and well clothed—their shoes hadn't even worn out. It looked like they were going to make it into the Promised Land after all; that is, until they received the undercover spy report.

Twelve spies were dispatched to check out conditions in the new land. Ten came back trembling and dejected after encountering the giants. True to their previous pattern, they complained all over again. They murmured against Moses and Aaron and bemoaned the fact that, according to their calculation, they were all going to die in the wilderness. They even accused God of bringing them to that desolate place in order to kill them.

As a result, God got pretty ticked off at their lack of faith and trust in him. He threatened to wipe out the whole nation and start over again with a new bunch of people. However, Moses interceded for them, and God relented. He didn't disinherit Israel, but the ones who murmured and complained died in the wilderness, just like they believed they would (see Num.13–14).

From that example, it is obvious murmuring and complaining is not the way to respond to unfavorable circumstances. So what is the right way?

Paul's Secret

Paul made an interesting statement in Philippians 4:11–12:

> I have learned how to be content (satisfied to the point where I am not disturbed or disquieted) in whatever state I am.
>
> I know how to be abased and live humbly in straitened circumstances, and I know also how to enjoy plenty and live in abundance. I have learned in any and all circumstances the secret of facing every situation, whether well-fed or going hungry, having a sufficiency and enough to spare or going without and being in want.

Paul had a secret; it was a secret he had learned. Maybe if we could learn his secret, we too could be content and not disturbed or disquieted no matter what circumstance we face.

In Philippians 4:4, he revealed the first part of his secret. His advice at the first sign of opposition or adverse circumstances was to *rejoice*.

"Rejoice in the Lord always [delight, gladden yourselves in Him]; again I say, Rejoice!"

You might say, "What does Paul know about a stack of unpaid bills, a broken down car, a washing machine that quits suddenly in the middle of wash day, children on drugs, a husband who is an alcoholic, and so on? If Paul had to deal with the problems I have, he wouldn't have anything to rejoice about."

Paul did not say to rejoice because you don't have any problems. Contrary to what some may think, Paul didn't even say to rejoice *because* of your problems. He simply said to rejoice in the Lord. How can you rejoice in the Lord when your problems are staring you in the face and seem overwhelming? He tells you how in part two of his secret: "Do not fret or have any anxiety about anything, but in every circumstance and in everything, by prayer and petition (definite requests), with thanksgiving, continue to make your wants known to God" (Phil. 4:6).

Paul could rejoice in the midst of adverse circumstances because he was acquainted with the *secret of prayer*. He understood a concept that he wanted to get across to us: There is no situation that God cannot change. There is nothing impossible with God A person who has an inexhaustible supply for every need, never really has a need.

Someone with a million dollars in the bank does not see a need for a hundred dollars as a problem because he knows he has an adequate supply to draw on. However, should he have just ten dollars in the bank but needs a hundred, that man has a problem.

Because Paul was convinced that God was his source of supply for whatever he needed, he could be filled with thanksgiving. A person who is confident that God will come through for him will be free from anxiety or agitation because he can cast his cares over on Him.

"Casting the whole of your care [all your anxieties, all your worries, all your concerns, once and for all] on Him, for He cares for you affectionately and cares about you watchfully" (1 Pet. 5:7).

Jailhouse Rock

Paul had a vision one night while he and Silas were trying to decide where to take their next missionary journey. He saw a man who beckoned him to come over to Macedonia and help them. Immediately, they endeavored to go there to preach the gospel to them.

When they arrived in Philippi, the chief city of Macedonia, a women's prayer group was the only people they found to minister to. Not long after that, they were thrown in prison for casting a demon out of a girl who was possessed with a spirit of divination. They were incarcerated, not in just any old part of the jail. Paul and Silas were thrust into the deepest darkest section. Their hands and feet were rammed into stocks, and their backs beaten to a bloody pulp. Under normal circumstances, their conversation could have gone something like this.

"Well, Silas," Paul might have mumbled, "do you think we missed God?"

Silas could have retorted, "I don't know Paul, but something sure is wrong. I thought you told me you saw a man in your vision, but so far, all we have seen is a bunch of women. Are you sure you saw a vision after all? It could have been something you ate, you know."

Paul and Silas could have spent the night not only bemoaning the fact that their feet and hands were going to sleep in those stocks, blaming each other, and ultimately murmuring and complaining against God. They could have bewailed the fact that their backs were killing them and groaned about the unbearable discomfort of the flies swarming around their raw flesh. They could have, but they didn't because Paul had a secret.

He had learned how to maintain peace in the midst of even severe trials and not get aggravated and angry. Instead of complaining and murmuring about their situation, Paul and Silas did what Paul told us to do. First of all, they prayed. Then, they rejoiced, not because they were in such a predicament but because they knew God was big enough to get them out.

In Acts 16:25, Paul and Silas sang praises to God so loud that the other prisoners heard them. Suddenly, the earth began to quake, the foundations of the prison shook, and miraculously, the prison doors opened. Every one of the prisoners' chains fell off, and they were free. As a result, the jail keeper was born again along with his whole family. Paul's secret had performed with accurate precision.

The Ten O'clock Flight

Many years ago, my husband and I had the privilege of taking a tour to Jordan and Israel, with Rome as our final stop. I had always dreamed of walking along the shores of Galilee where Jesus and his disciples had walked, and true to my expectations, the trip proved exciting. But when we arrived in Rome, we had grown a little weary. The mothers who had been away from their children for almost two weeks were getting homesick, and I was one of them.

The day we were to depart from Rome, we were told that our departure would be delayed one more day because of a strike at the airport. Disappointed, frustrated and dejected, we plodded through the day anticipating the next day's departure. At 4:30 a.m. the following morning, our group headed for Rome airport.

When we arrived, we were kept standing in an over-crowded lobby for what seemed like hours. We glanced nervously at our watches because we could see it was getting closer and closer to the time we were supposed to board our plane. Still, no one told us to line up for inspection.

Finally, to our dismay, they informed us there was a strong possibility we would not get a flight that day at all. The airlines were honoring tickets purchased for that day only. All tickets purchased for the previous day were put on standby. We surveyed the overflowing lobby with a sinking feeling where hundreds of people milled around waiting to board the available flights.

Everywhere we turned, we heard angry travelers grumbling and complaining, and personally, I wanted to sit down and have a good cry. Then I remembered Paul's secret: first, pray; next, rejoice; and finally, enjoy God's peace in your mind and heart. Since Charlie was busy with the luggage, I found a lady I had met who I knew to be a woman of faith.

I pulled her aside and whispered, "Do I ever have a prayer project for you!"

She and I had a prayer meeting right there in the Rome airport, and we didn't care who saw us. As we prayed, we detected the still small voice of the Holy Spirit. He reminded us of the children of Israel who had come to the Red Sea and found they had no way of escape, but God supernaturally made a way for them. We had a strong impression that he was going to make a way for us too.

Instead of going around saying, "Woe is me. It looks like we are never going to get home." We said over and over again, "Praise the Lord! We are going home."

Jesus promised in Matthew 18:19: "If two shall agree on earth as touching anything that they shall ask, it shall be done for them of my Father which is in heaven." On the basis of that promise, the two of us agreed that the ten o'clock flight would not leave without us. Because we believed, we were convinced that when the ten o'clock flight left, we would be on that plane.

When ten o'clock came and went, we gritted our teeth and kept on rejoicing. Circumstances looked like our prayers were not going to be answered, but because God's word said our Heavenly Father would answer our prayers, we kept on rejoicing.

Twelve o'clock came. Finally, the announcement we had been waiting for came. Thirty of our group could prepare to board a plane. My prayer partner, her husband, and Charlie and I were among the thirty who were chosen. Several hours later, we boarded the most beautiful airplane we had ever seen. As it prepared to take off at approximately 6:00 p.m., they announced that this flight had been previously scheduled to leave at *ten o'clock that morning!* Obviously, they were a little late in departing, but they hadn't been able to take off earlier because they couldn't leave without us.

When Paul revealed his secret, he was not trying to be super spiritual by saying, "When things get tough, brother, just praise the Lord. It will make you feel better." No. Paul knew it was to our advantage to trust God. He wanted us to know that griping and complaining will change *nothing*, but faith in God's ability can change *anything!*

The beautiful result of practicing Paul's secret is the ability to experience and maintain God's peace. If I had known about this wonderful secret on that difficult day at the ranch, when each successive challenge arose, I could have prayed and cast my cares on Jesus. As a result, those pesky problems would not have caused frustrations; they would have produced prayer requests instead. I could have started the day wrapped in peace and then successfully maintained God's peace all day long instead of becoming frustrated, jumpy, and wasting time behaving like a raving maniac.

Paul finished explaining his secret by revealing its rewarding outcome: "And God's peace [shall be yours, that tranquil state of a soul assured of its salvation through Christ, and so fearing nothing from God and being content with its earthly lot of whatever sort that is, that peace] which transcends all understanding shall garrison and mount guard over your hearts and minds in Christ Jesus" (Phil. 4:7).

As I shared my story of a day in the life of a rancher's wife with all its ugly details, you may have noticed that even though my husband had nothing to do with the circumstances I faced that day, he experienced the brunt of my anger. I wasn't angry at him, I was just angry. But anger has to be vented, so once the fuse is lit, there is going to be an explosion. That's why maintaining peace in the midst of negative circumstances is so important in relationships. Aggravation is the breeding ground for strife. If one person gets upset in a relationship, she is bound to take it out on the other.

So getting aggravated at *circumstances* can be deadly to relationships, but then there is the other source of aggravation. *People* aggravate us. Now that's another matter altogether.

Living with Porcupines

Unhappy individuals who habitually become aggravated are like porcupines. Porcupines are fascinating creatures that look harmless enough as they amble through life, minding their own business, but when something riles them, watch out. You might get hurt.

There are people like that. If they don't like the way you behave, they get aggravated with you. That mind-set is so firmly embedded and so much a part of their outlook that it's hard to convince them they have a choice about getting aggravated. They are certain that they have a right, even a duty, to feel that way. You can see how that can be especially harmful to relationships.

Anytime you get aggravated at someone, you are saying, "It's all about me. I really don't care about you." This brings us back to the original law of human relationships—the law of love. It's apparent that every quill of a porcupine-type person is securely rooted in the body of selfishness.

Previously, we found that the aggravation aroused by challenging circumstances destroys our peace. Aggravation that arises as a result of imperfections, inconsistencies, or immaturity in individuals comes from *impatience*.

You need a healthy supply of patience in order to live in peace with flawed people—they are everywhere, even looking back at you from the mirror. When the word *patience* is used in regard to relationships, it means long-suffering or forbearance.

The definition of *long-suffering* is "enduring the injuries of offense for a long time without complaining, this includes forbearance toward the faults or infirmities of others, all the while possessing a quiet tolerant fortitude under distress or annoyance."

You may not be familiar with the word *forbearance*. It's described as "refraining from claiming or enforcing a right, and abstaining from retaliation or retribution."

To keep from getting aggravated at irritating people, you must allow the fruit of patience to grow so you can develop forbearance.

Paul writes in Colossians 3:12–14:

> Clothe yourselves therefore, as God's own chosen ones (His own picked representatives)...by putting on behavior marked by tenderhearted pity and mercy, kind feeling, a lowly opinion of yourselves, gentle ways, [and] *patience [which is tireless and long-suffering, and has the power to endure whatever comes, with good temper]*. (emphasis mine)
>
> Be gentle and forbearing with one another and, if one has a difference (a grievance or complaint) against another, readily pardoning each other; even as the Lord has [freely] forgiven you, so must you also [forgive]. And above all these [put on] love and enfold yourselves with the bond of perfectness [which binds everything together completely in ideal harmony].

Peace and happiness are never going to come about because of a perfect relationship, but come because you choose to be patient in the face of imperfections and continue to love. Let's face it, people are imperfect creatures. It's unrealistic to expect perfection; so you are advised to put on or clothe yourself with patience, long-suffering, and forbearance and keep on loving.

God is patient with people because he sees them not as imperfect and flawed individuals but as unfinished. Anyone can find character defects and performance flaws in another person. It takes the grace of God to look beyond an impulsive Peter to see a rock of the church or look beyond Saul the persecutor and see Paul the apostle. Being patient takes work and involves seeing like God sees.

When my children were born, the ugly trait of impatience began to emerge in my life. I wasn't used to having little people around with all their limitations and needs, so in those early years, I'm sure I was unpleasant to live with.

I was unhappy with my behavior because I had been under the thumb of impatient people before and knew how hurtful it was, but I couldn't seem to help myself. One day, while praying about this problem, the Lord reminded me that patience was one of the fruit of the spirit, and it is the very nature of fruit to grow. Because patience is a fruit of the Holy Spirit, and he is inside me, then all the fruit are there as well. However, getting those characteristics exhibited on the outside takes a bit of doing.

Like love, patience was deposited in your inner man when you were born again, but it must be allowed to come out in the same way you turn on your faucet of love; it's a choice of your will.

When I came to that realization, I determined to become a patient person. The only way I knew how to start was simply to act like I was patient, much like an actor depicts a character quite unlike himself. At first, it was grit my teeth, clamp my mouth shut, and ignore all those familiar agitated feelings stirring on the inside. After days and months of consistently doing that, something wonderful started to happen. It wasn't a teeth-gritting, mouth-clamping experience anymore; I actually felt patient and loving and forbearing. Before I knew it, long-suffering became a lifestyle.

My children have no idea how close they came to having to grow up with a porcupine. Who knows where my life would have ended up if I hadn't stumbled onto the key to unlock patience?

If you happen to live with a porcupine, the key to survival is to put on the armor of light (love) for protection that Romans 13:12 describes. Study the chapters on offense and forgiveness to see how to dress yourself in this defensive apparel. Peter says in 1 Peter 3:13, "Now who is there to hurt you if you are zealous followers of that which is good?"

And, if you have discovered you are a porcupine, do us a favor. Let the fruit of patience grow. Then little by little your quills will fall out, and you will become quite harmless and pleasant to live with.

9

Ingrown Eyeballs

Over the years, I have had the privilege of teaching seminars in various places. After one particular service, a lady grabbed my arm and exclaimed rather sheepishly, "I sure needed to hear what you had to say about self-pity. I had developed a bad case of 'ingrown eyeballs'!"

She came up with one of the best definitions for self-pity I have heard. Self-pity is exactly as it sounds; it's all about self. It is pure selfishness wrapping its nasty shroud around your attitude, encasing you in gloom, doom, agony, deep dark depression, and excessive misery—as the characters on the show *Hee Haw* lamented many years ago. Self-pity has the effect of turning any potentially pleasant situation into a litany of negativity twisting even the sunniest day into one of darkness and foreboding.

A more clinical description of *self-pity* is "the feeling of grief or pain awakened by the misfortunes or sorrows that occur in one's own life as a result of an undue regard for one's own interest; or an overdue and exclusive care for one's own comfort and pleasure, with little regard for the happiness and often the rights of others." It is the God-given compassion that we should have for others turned inward toward ourselves.

I have to confess, one of the most prominent flaws in my temperament is the tendency to indulge in moments—no, I have to be honest—days of self-pity. Once I start that downward decent into the pit of self-pity, it gets hard to climb out without a great deal of effort.

There was a period in my life when each day was a succession of pity parties. (A pity party is an event when you and the devil buddy up and cry on each other's shoulder while he reinforces the thought that you have every right to feel sorry for yourself.) During that particular time, I had a dream. I was in a pasture standing ankle-deep in some horrible, slimy, stinky substance. You might be able to figure out what the stinky substance was by where it was located. It was so revolting in appearance and smell that it was nauseating. Even though it was repulsive, I had an overpowering compulsion to scoop some up.

With it dripping from my hands, I heard a smooth, persuasive voice whisper, "Rub your face in it."

As disgusting as it was, I had an overwhelming urge to do what the voice suggested. As though hypnotized, I started to bring the nasty slime to my face. But then something inside rose up and I flung it away shouting, "No! I don't have to rub my face in this stuff, and I won't!"

I awoke with a start. The dream had been so vivid and had affected me in such a dramatic way that I knew it must have a meaning. When I asked the Lord to show me its significance, he spoke to my spirit, "That loathsome stuff you were surrounded with was self-pity. The devil wants you to wallow in it, and you have been complying with his wishes. Self-pity is as disgusting to me as that repulsive slime was to you in your dream. Cast it off as violently as you did in your dream."

What I didn't understand then is why God hates self-pity so much. Now, I have come to realize that self-pity and faith cannot rule a person's life at the same time. When you feel sorry for yourself, you have no faith. When that's the case, not only are you a prime target for the enemy's attacks, but you cannot please God either.

Hebrews 11:6 reads, "But without faith it is impossible to please and be satisfactory to Him."

God wants the very best for you. However, when you are filled with self-pity, the devil is able to infiltrate your world with his stealing, killing, and destroying plots, messing up the glorious plans and blessings God has for you.

In Ephesians 6:16, when Paul taught about the armor of God, he wasn't just giving a nice little Bible lesson. He revealed an all-important battle strategy. During spiritual warfare, one of the most important items necessary to win a convincing victory over Satan is the *shield of faith*. With it, you are able to quench all the fiery darts of the wicked one.

What happens if you lay down that vital piece of equipment? You become vulnerable to the devil's arsenal of weapons and are primed for defeat. That's what self-pity does. It strips you of your shield of faith. All you have left is a runny nose and bleary eyes from crying and feeling sorry for yourself, and consequently, your situation never changes.

To get any difficult situation fixed requires ability greater than the energy you release through whining and complaining. You need the power of God. To release his miraculous transforming strength into your negative circumstances requires faith. Faith, and faith alone, moves the hand of God. You can gripe and grumble all you want to other people and even to God, but it will never make any difference. Faith changes things. Self-pity ties God's hands and limits his ability to work on your behalf. That's why he hates self-pity.

Even though feeling sorry for yourself never alters your challenging circumstances, it does affect your life. A list of what self-pity accomplishes includes

- depression
- physical weakness
- a negative outlook on life
- hopelessness
- strife and contention in relationships
- bitterness
- withdrawal from social situations
- lack of spiritual vision
- ungratefulness
- murmuring, complaining and misery
- destroys patience during trials and nullifies long-suffering

None of these symptoms add quality to our lives, so why are we so prone to indulge in self-pity when conditions get tough? Maybe because we think we don't have a choice.

It's All About the Attitude

It's not *circumstances* or *mistreatment* that triggers self-pity, it's your *attitude*. You may not be able to control what happens to you, but you are in charge of your attitude.

The children of Israel had been miraculously delivered from a cruel life of slavery. Through a promise from God, they were given the keys to a brand new future in a land abounding with milk and honey. All they had to do was trust God along the way and keep their attitude straight and bingo! New life, new land! That didn't happen however, stuff happened, and instead of pressing on in faith, they bellyached about everything that made them uncomfortable. To say the least, God was not pleased. "And they journeyed from Mount Hor by the way to the Red Sea, to go around the land of Edom, and the people became impatient (depressed, much discouraged), because [of the trials] of the way" (Num. 21:4). "And the people grumbled and deplored their hardships, which was evil in the ears of the Lord, and when the Lord heard it, His anger was kindled" (Num. 11:1).

Those people probably thought they were just telling it like it was, just unloading or venting to each other, but God was listening. You may be able to hide your attitude from some folks, but you can't conceal it from God. It's one thing for your friends or spouse to get angry, but when God's anger is kindled, watch out. Things are fixing to get serious. Self-pity may be an option for you, but to God, it is a major slap in his face and evil in his ears.

Some attitudes that breed self-pity are

1. It's awful if I have to suffer in any way, before my prayers are answered or I reach my goal, and so on;

2. It's awful if I have to wait;

3. It's awful if I have to put forth any effort to bring about changes. (For example: forgive, walk in love, go the extra mile, and so on);

4. No one or nothing has a right to inconvenience me;

5. My needs and desires must be met in order for me to be happy;

6. Nobody knows, or cares, or is helping me. Someone or something else is to blame, not me, so there is nothing I can do about it.

Those are just a few embedded patterns of thought that precondition you to become infected with self-pity, and they all sprout from selfishness.

Bad Attitudes Stink

A few years ago, our son Brad and his wife Tamy came to our house to visit along with their family and two inside dogs. By *inside*, I mean dogs that spend most of their time in the house. That's always an adjustment for us since we keep all our animals outside. However, because we love our kids, we love their dogs too.

The last night of their stay, Balto and Molly, the dogs, were running around outside having a wonderful time when we heard a ruckus at the back door. Tamy flung open the door only to be blasted in the nostrils with the disgusting odor of a skunk (probably the same one I had spied sometime earlier in the gazebo). In through the open door bounded the two dogs, reeking with the foul-smelling aroma. They had experienced their first head to tail confrontation with a skunk and lived to regret it.

Both dogs did the only thing dogs know to do. They rubbed their contaminated bodies all over the living room carpet trying to get rid of the tormenting odor. Brad whisked Balto and Molly to the bathtub for a thorough and immediate dog wash, but it was too late. The sickening odor had already penetrated the atmosphere in our house from top to bottom.

We did everything we could to change the smell in our house. I pulled out every candle I had purchased from fund-raising drives our youth had promoted over the years. We positioned them in various places around the house and hoped for the best, but days and even weeks later, we could still detect the residue of that encounter with the stinking rotten smell of that skunk.

Bad attitudes have a way of polluting the atmosphere wherever they are. Self-pity is a frame of mind that stinks, and it's quite evident no matter where you encounter it. It reminds me of Pigpen in the Charlie Brown cartoons who constantly traveled with a cloud surrounding him. I never knew whether it was a cloud of dust or a telltale odor that clung to him. Nevertheless, wherever he went, it went.

We can change clothes, jobs, and even locations; but whatever we do and wherever we go, if we don't change our outlook on life, our bad attitudes will go with us, polluting our environment and deflecting any happiness that might venture our way.

Self-pity Produces Depression

Many in the medical profession have detected a chemical imbalance in the brains of those who suffer from depression; therefore, they believe the solution is to give the patient a drug that will correct the chemical distortion. However, when thoughts of self-pity are allowed in our lives for very long, depression is always the result. Many suffering individuals are popping a pill for depression when what they need is to scrutinize their thought patterns instead.

Dr. Leaf, who has extensively researched the human brain, states in her book, *Who Switched off My Brain*, "Every thought has a corresponding electrochemical reaction in your brain; when you think, chemicals course through your body in magnificently complex electrochemical feedback loops. When you feel happy, your brain has released specific types of chemicals or neurotransmitters called endorphins or *feel-good chemicals*. The brain releases endorphins in response to pleasurable thoughts.

"But when you feel sad, afraid, angry or hopeless, your brain releases different types of chemicals. Depending on whether or not your emotions are toxic to your body, the chemicals will either help you or harm you. Research shows that around 87% of illnesses can be attributed to your thought life, whereas approximately 13% to diet, genetics and environment."

She further declares that researchers have conceded for years that the role of fear, anger, depression, anxiety and a variety of other emotions play a role in causing mental and physical health problems. The medical field's solution to this problem has been to develop pharmaceutical drugs aimed at trying to change the brain's chemistry to make us feel good.

"We don't need any more of these *happy pills*," Dr. Leaf says. "What we need are coping strategies to help us avoid the problems before they come up and detox our minds and bodies of the toxic thoughts that are already causing damage. The good news is that these coping strategies are readily available and quickly accessible. You don't have to travel far to find them, and they won't cost a fortune. They begin with a thought and your reactions to the thoughts that go on inside your head."

Make Yourself Save Yourself

In the wilderness of Judah, a day's journey from Beersheba, a lone figure collapsed under a desolate juniper tree, exhausted and spent from his grueling eighty-mile trip. Elijah, shaken by Queen Jezebel's threats against his life, had hastily fled the land of Israel.

Days before, he had confronted the occult leaders of his time, and as a result, he experienced an overwhelming victory when supernatural fire came down from heaven. Shortly thereafter, he carried out the execution of the prophets of Baal, and as a result of his intercession, a deluge of rain broke a three-and-a-half–year drought. But now, that was all a distant memory. Elijah was depressed. So much so, in fact, that out of the depths of his despair, he wailed, "It is enough; now, O lord, take away my life" (1 Kings 19:4).

You would think after such an uncommon demonstration of the power of God, Elijah would stay exhilarated for a long time and that it would take more than the threats of a mere earthly queen to send him into a tailspin of self-pity and discouragement.

A scenario of this sort happens more often than we like to admit. Anyone who has been in ministry long knows that the greater the victory, the more apt there is to be a fierce counterattack from the enemy. More often than not, that attack comes in the form of lies and half-truths aimed at our thought life. Satan's purpose is always to discourage the saints of God. He tries to convince them they have failed in some way, endeavoring to persuade them to just give up the fight and pray to die.

Several times, I have had run-ins with this crushing spirit of discouragement. I discovered that no matter how long you walk with God or how knowledgeable you think you are of Satan's devices, you are never immune from these attacks—especially when you desire to go to a higher level in your spiritual life.

In the middle of one those assaults, after spending hours in a pit of self-pity and deep depression, I finally tried to pray and hear from God. All I heard was, "And David encouraged himself in the Lord" (1 Sam. 30:6).

That was not exactly what I wanted to hear because frankly, I didn't think I had the strength to do anything for myself. What I really wanted was for someone else to encourage me and do the work for me. After a few feeble attempts to turn my thought life from a hopelessly negative point of view to a more optimistic outlook, I heard the Spirit of God speak to my spirit. "Did you think you could move to a higher level spiritually and not be contested by the adversary?"

He reminded me of the scripture in Matthew 11:12 where Jesus said, "And from the days of John the Baptist until the present time, the kingdom of heaven has endured violent assault, and violent men seize it by force [as a precious prize—a share in the heavenly kingdom is sought with most ardent zeal and intense exertion]."

That's when I knew my victory was up to me, not someone else, and I suspected it was going to take *intense* effort. A friend once told me that when you lose your joy and get depressed, you are going to have to *make yourself save yourself*. A wimp is never going to be an overcomer. It takes determined strength to fight for the higher life in the kingdom of God.

The adversary is never going to just sit passively by and let you gain ground spiritually. He will oppose you at every turn. One of the most effective weapons he uses is discouragement and self-pity. The outcome of discouragement is always depression. That's when your spirit is so pressed down that instead of enthusiastically pressing into the good things that God has made available, you are tempted to lie down and quit.

During that particular bout with the adversary, I received this word from the Lord about discouragement.

"If you bow your knee to discouragement, despair, or depression, you have bowed your knee to the god of this world who can sometimes control circumstances. However, if you refuse to bow your knee to discouragement, you have bowed and submitted yourself to me, the Almighty God of the universe, who has the power to overcome all circumstances. You cannot control circumstances, but you can choose who you bow your knee to."

You may encounter circumstances throughout your life that blindside and threaten to overwhelm, or maybe you are in a challenging situation that looks like it's never going to change. In those times, it is vital to do what David did when he was tempted to get in self-pity and discouragement. Instead of wallowing in depression, he took the initiative and encouraged himself in the Lord. Psalms 43:5 is an example of how he talked himself right out of the pit.

"Why go I mourning because of the oppression of the enemy? Why are you cast down, O my inner self? And why should you moan over me and be disquieted within me? Hope in God and wait expectantly for Him, for I shall yet praise Him, Who is the help of my [sad] countenance, and my God" (Ps. 43: 2, 5).

When the spirit of self-pity rears its ugly head, it is important who you talk to and what you say. *Stop* moaning and complaining to God about your big problems; instead, inform your problems that *you've got a big God.*

So You Think You've Got It Bad

How do you get rid of the stench of self-pity? Does it happen because finally all your circumstances even out, your comfort returns, and everything is going your way? If only we had even one whole day like that, let alone a lifetime, it would be wonderful. The bad news is: life is filled with hardships. The good news is: those challenges don't have to affect your attitude. If you keep your outlook free from the contamination of self-pity, they will only refine and define your purpose and turn you into an overcomer. It all depends on your thought life.

Paul the apostle was a prime example of an overcomer who learned how to control his thoughts and attitudes. If ever there was someone who had a right to feel sorry for himself, he did. In 2 Corinthians 11: 23–28, he gave an inventory of all the adversity he had to go through.

In addition to extensive labor, imprisonment, being beaten and brought to the point of death, five times he received forty lashes from a whip, three times he was beaten with rods, once he was stoned, and he was wrecked at sea on three different occasions. Besides that, he encountered numerous perils. Perils from rivers, bandits, and perils everywhere he went—in the city, desert places, the sea, and even from those posing as believers. On top of all that, sometimes he went hungry and experienced thirst. He also knew what it was like to be cold and exposed to the elements with very little clothing.

Then he added the clincher in verse twenty-eight: "And besides those things that are without, there is the daily [inescapable pressure] of my care and anxiety for all the churches."

Just listing those difficulties makes me feel sorry for Paul, so it's a wonder he didn't just throw in the towel and call it quits after the first few perils. But he didn't. In 2 Corinthians 4:8–9, Paul gave us his victory statement: "We are hedged in (pressed) on every side [troubled and oppressed in every way], but not cramped or crushed; we suffer embarrassments and are perplexed and unable to find a way out, but not driven to despair; we are pursued (persecuted and hard driven), but not deserted [to stand alone]; we are struck down to the ground, but never struck out and destroyed."

Well now, that's good news, but what kept Paul from being smothered with self-pity? If we examine the epistles he wrote during those times in his life, we find out how he sidestepped the pit of self-pity, and we can do the same.

First of all, Paul said he never allowed himself the luxury of yielding to his flesh. He made this statement in Acts 24:16: "Therefore I always exercise and discipline myself [mortifying my body, deadening my carnal affections, bodily appetites, and worldly desires, endeavoring in all respects] to have a clear (unshaken, blameless) conscience, void of offense toward God and toward men."

In times of difficulties, there is always the temptation to get mad at the people who are causing you pain or get offended at God, whom you might mistakenly conclude is allowing all those unpleasant things to happen. Doing that stirs up your flesh and allows selfishness to take over. Thus, self-pity is the first little imp that barges through the door. You then find yourself teetering on the slippery edge of the pit.

Second Corinthians 4, tells us Paul's complete strategy. In verse thirteen, he revealed one of the most important habits he carried out at the very onset. Instead of murmuring and complaining, he routinely spoke words of faith. "Yet we have the same spirit of faith as he had who wrote, I have believed, and therefore have I spoken. We too believe, and therefore we speak."

Right in the middle of the storms of life, Paul clung determinedly to his shield of faith, not allowing it to be stripped from him by the enemy.

Next, he revealed the rest of his course of action in verses sixteen to eighteen:

> Therefore we do not become discouraged (utterly spiritless, exhausted, and wearied out through fear). Though our outer man is [progressively] decaying and wasting away, yet our inner self is being [progressively] renewed day after day.
>
> For our light, momentary affliction (this slight distress of the passing hour) is ever more and more abundantly preparing and producing and achieving for us an everlasting weight of glory [beyond all measure, excessively surpassing all comparisons and all calculations, a vast and transcendent glory and blessedness never to cease!],
>
> Since we consider and look not to the things that are seen but to the things that are unseen; for the things that are visible are temporal (brief and fleeting), but the things that are invisible are deathless and everlasting.

Embedded in those scriptures is the information Paul used to maintain an excellent attitude no matter what came his way. In every situation he *trusted* God to turn the situation around for his good, and believed the outcome would be for his glory. Because his focus was on the eternal purpose of his life and ministry, he was convinced that his situation was momentary, temporal, and subject to change. He then strengthened his inner man, not by griping and complaining, but by expecting his circumstances to get better.

> For I am well assured and indeed know that through your prayers and a bountiful supply of the Spirit of Jesus Christ (the Messiah) this will turn out for my preservation (for the spiritual health and welfare of my own soul) and avail toward the saving work of the Gospel. This is in keeping with my own eager desire and persistent expectation and hope. (Phil.1:19–20)

I believe Paul's inspiration during negative circumstances came from the example of Jesus Christ himself. Jesus was despised and rejected by men. Even though he was, in fact, royalty of the highest degree, never having done even one thing wrong, he was horribly mistreated, misunderstood, and finally cruelly crucified.

But he never gave in to self-pity. Hebrews 12:2 reveals, "He, for the joy [of obtaining the prize] that was set before Him, endured the cross, despising and ignoring the shame, and is now seated at the right hand of the throne of God."

Jesus had the same ability that Paul talked about. They both knew where to focus their attention. Paul looked at those things that were in the eternal realm and Jesus kept his eyes on the joy of obtaining the prize. What do you suppose that prize was? Part of it was to be seated at the right hand of the Father once again, but I can't help but think the prize he referred to was the blood-bought, born again children he would redeem who would get to sit beside him in heavenly places—that includes you and me. If Jesus had died in self-pity, the faith he needed to be raised from the dead would have been stripped away, and we would still be in our sins.

> Since we are surrounded by so great a cloud of witnesses [who have borne testimony to the Truth], let us strip off and throw aside every encumbrance (unnecessary weight) and that sin which so readily (deftly and cleverly) clings to and entangles us, and let us run with patient endurance and steady and active persistence the appointed course of the race that is set before us,
>
> Looking away [from all that will distract] to Jesus, Who is the Leader and the Source of our faith [giving the first incentive for our belief] and is also its Finisher [bringing it to maturity and perfection].
>
> Just think of Him Who endured from sinners such grievous opposition and bitter hostility against Himself [reckon up and consider it all in comparison with your trials], so that you may not grow weary or exhausted, losing heart and relaxing and fainting in your minds. You have not yet struggled and fought agonizingly against sin, nor have you yet resisted and withstood to the point of pouring out your [own] blood. (Hebrews 12:1–4)

Compared to Paul and Jesus, we don't have it so bad. We might as well quit bellyaching and complaining. Fling away that horrible, stinking self-pity that drags us down to the pit of despair. Get those ingrown eyeballs off ourselves, and see the needs of someone else. Turn compassion away from our own selfish little world, and let it flow out to others the way God intended. Then, the aroma of our lives won't smell so awful.

"All the days of the desponding and afflicted are made evil [by anxious thoughts and forebodings], but he who has a glad heart has a continual feast [regardless of circumstances]" (Prov. 15:15).

10

Dealing with Criticism

Fred Allen, an American comedian, once said: "If criticism had any power, the skunk would be extinct a long time ago." It's true. Critical words have no real power, but criticism is not harmless. "Sticks and stones may break my bones, but words will never harm me" is not in the Bible. Words have the ability to damage in a more permanent way than a beating with a ball bat or an avalanche of rocks. Broken bones will heal, but criticism has the ability to rip a person open inside and shatter her self-image creating wounds that can fester for a lifetime.

Relationships and homes that should be solid and healthy can be shredded and demolished forever as a result of a critical or judgmental spirit. A few negative words that castigate have the ability to demoralize not just a home but a vision, a mission, or an individual.

Jesus warned in Matthew 12:25, "Any kingdom that is divided against itself is being brought to desolation and laid waste, and no city or house divided against itself will last or continue to stand." Mark confirms this in Mark 3:25: "And if a house is divided (split into factions and rebelling) against itself, that house will not be able to last."

We know what it's like to be criticized—and probably have dished out a healthy portion ourselves—but to better understand it, I'm going to give the definition. To be critical means "to give severe judgment, finding fault or carping, to examine carefully and then to judge."

We don't use the word *carping* much, so I'll include that meaning—it's "finding fault unreasonably, complaining, picking out flaws or raising trivial objections."

If I hadn't added that last definition, maybe we could have escaped unscathed. We might have convinced ourselves that we are not critical, but just being honest. However, when we throw in the mix "complaining and picking out flaws," we would have to hang our heads and admit we're guilty.

It's characteristic of human nature to "carp," probably because its source is the original sin, pride. When sin deposited that trait in our first parents, they passed it on to the next generation, and from then on, each subsequent generation became infected. Pride is one of the seven things on God's hate list as recorded in Proverbs 6:17: "A proud look (the spirit that makes one overestimate himself and underestimate others)."

The individual who is critical ranks his opinion above the person he criticizes. He is saying, "I am right, and he or she is wrong," thus elevating himself above the other person, fitting the description of someone who overestimates himself.

The Mirror of Criticism

The story is told of a man and an angel who were walking along together. The man was complaining about his neighbors. "I never saw such a wretched set of people as are in this village," he said. "They are mean, greedy, selfish, and careless of the needs of others. Worst of all, they are forever speaking evil of one another."

"Is that so?" asked the angel.

"It is, indeed," said the man. "Why, only look at this fellow coming toward us. I know his face though I cannot remember his name. See his little sharklike, cruel eyes, darting here and there like a ferret's, and the lines of hardness about his mouth. The very droop of his shoulders is mean and cringing, and he slinks along instead of walking."

"It is very clever of you to see all this," said the angel. "But there is one thing you did not perceive—that is a mirror we are approaching."

This story exposes one of the central truths in regard to criticism. We are more prone to notice the faults in others that we *have* in our own lives, especially if we haven't faced them and dealt with them ourselves. Paul writes about this tendency in Romans 2:1: "Therefore you have no excuse or defense or justification, O man, whoever you are who judges and condemns another. For in posing as judge and passing sentence on another, you condemn yourself, because you who judge are habitually practicing the very same things [that you censure and denounce]. [But] we know that the judgment (adverse verdict, sentence) of God falls justly and in accordance with truth upon those who practice such things."

This verse warns that when you judge and condemn another person and practice the same thing you criticize others for, what you have to look forward to is judgment and an adverse verdict that you justly deserve.

"For just as you judge and criticize and condemn others, you will be judged and criticized and condemned, and in accordance with the measure you [use to] deal out to others, it will be dealt out again to you" (Matt. 7:2).

If you show mercy toward other people's faults, then you will receive mercy for yours. On the other hand, if you criticize others for their shortcomings, watch out. You are going to have some stones thrown at you for your failures. Sowing and reaping is not just about money. This principle works on every level of existence, especially relationships.

Who's the Judge?

James 5:9 warns, "Do not complain, brethren, against one another, so that you [yourselves] may not be judged. Look! The Judge is [already] standing at the very door."

The reason God hates criticizing and judging so much—besides the fact that it destroys unity and every godly relationship—is because when you are involved in this practice, you assume you know what is in another person's heart, and in reality, only God can look on the heart. God, "The Judge," knows when you are trying to be "a judge," and he will judge you according to the sentence you have rendered for someone else.

"One only is the Lawgiver and Judge Who is able to save and to destroy [the One Who has the absolute power of life and death]. [But you] who are you that [you presume to] pass judgment on your neighbor?" (James 4:12).

In Romans 14:4, Paul makes it clear that we have no business interfering with God's issues in regard to dealing with his servants: "Who are you to pass judgment on and censure another's household servant? It is before his own master that he stands or falls. And he shall stand and be upheld, for the Master (the Lord) is mighty to support him and make him stand."

The Message Bible says: "If there are corrections to be made or manners to be learned, God can handle that without your help."

Angel of Light

We are inclined to judge ourselves by our *intentions*, but we have a tendency to judge others by their *actions*. We often have supernatural help in seeing the faults of others. Second Corinthians 11:14 describes Satan as a master deceiver who *masquerades as an angel of light*. His tactic is to blind our eyes to *our own faults* and give outstanding revelations and insight into the *faults of others*. Then he puts pressure on us to confront that seriously flawed person with the intention of correcting or pointing out to them the error of their ways. More often than not, this only causes hurt, misunderstanding, resentment, and division, then unfortunately, our crusade ends up backfiring on us.

Dale Carnegie said, "Criticism is futile because it puts a man on the defensive and usually makes him strive to justify himself. Criticism is dangerous because it wounds a man's precious pride, hurts his sense of importance, and arouses his resentment."

Satan loves it when he can accomplish these things in an individual; therefore, his favorite scenario is exposé. His greatest desire is to make public all the delicious flaws a person might have to as many people as he can. His intent is to cause insurmountable damage and pain, leaving along the way a trail of damaged reputations and shattered relationships. It's no wonder a critical spirit has free reign in our midst; the devil deceives us into thinking we are doing God a favor by judging—helping him out so to speak. In reality, we are not helping God out at all; instead, we are helping the devil do his job of destroying.

God doesn't need our help because for the most part, our motives are wrong. Criticism comes from the spirit that makes us overestimate ourselves and underestimate others, so it can never produce the power to change behavior. When God brings correction, he does it with the intent of helping his children grow. In fact, we just read in Romans 14:4 that God is *mighty to support* every one of his servants—even those who have genuine faults—and he is determined to supply them with all the help they need so they can stand and not fall.

God's Official Helpers

There are many people who have a critical spirit perched on their shoulder who go about as self-appointed judges, criticizing everyone they meet, especially those in authority over them. As crusaders, they are unaware that their commission does not come from God but is instigated by the accuser of the brethren himself.

If we are not supposed to correct other people's faults, how is God ever going to get the job done? Does he miraculously appear before a defective person and personally instruct or correct? Very seldom does it happen that way. God could use that method if he wanted to, but most of the time, he chooses another more practical delivery system. He speaks through individuals whom he has anointed and placed in positions of authority.

Ephesians 4:11 gives the lineup of those individuals who have appointed offices in the body of Christ. We call them the fivefold ministries, which include evangelists, pastors, apostles, prophets, and teachers. Verse twelve tells us why these people were placed in the church: "His intention was the perfecting and the full equipping of the saints (His consecrated people), [that they should do] the work of ministering toward building up Christ's body (the church)."

When a minister speaks under the inspiration of the Holy Spirit, it is as though God himself is speaking, and the message he brings is for the purpose of "instruction, reproof and conviction of sin, for correction of error and discipline in obedience, and for training in righteousness, so that the man of God may be complete and proficient, well-fitted and thoroughly equipped for every good work" (2 Tim. 3:16–17). This is for the purpose of building up the church, not tear it down—which is what criticism does.

Criticizing those in authority can cause serious problems. Just ask Aaron and Miriam. In Numbers 12, Miriam and Aaron talked against Moses because of his wife. They decided between themselves that Moses was no more qualified to lead their nation than they were. But they didn't realize the Lord was listening.

That's a little sobering, because most often when we discuss the faults of ministries over lunch, we think it's confidential, just between the two of us, and we are not aware there is a third party listening in. God hears those little digs—which now we know is carping—and he gets extremely ticked about it, setting in motion severe consequences. After God reprimanded Miriam and Aaron, when his presence departed, Miriam discovered she had leprosy. During the seven days she suffered with the disease, the progress of whole nation of Israel had to be put on hold until the situation was healed.

Groundbreaking Punishment

A little while later, even after the chastisement meted out to Aaron and Miriam, four guys named Korah, Dathan, Abiram, and On still didn't get it. They too began to criticize, not only Moses but Aaron as well. It wasn't just a whisper campaign they instigated, but a full-fledged board meeting made up of 250 princes and leaders of the congregation. This self-appointed committee accused their two God-appointed leaders of acting holier-than-thou and threatened to take over.

If you think God overdid it with Miriam, what he did to those rebels will shake you up a bit. One could say the repercussions were earth shattering. The ground opened and swallowed up the offenders and their families. In the process, God gave a severe warning to the rest of the congregation in Numbers 16:26. He said, "To depart from the tents of those wicked men, and to touch nothing of theirs, lest they be consumed in all their sins."

Sometimes, we secretly wish those who criticize us would disappear as dramatically as those rebels did in Moses's day; however, at some time or other, each of us has fallen into the category of harshly judging someone who is in authority. If the earth opened up and sucked out the offender every time a leader was criticized, we would already be gone.

Even though the earth doesn't split every time someone criticizes a minister or a person in authority, there are still some negative consequences. In John 6:66, when the followers of Jesus disapproved of one of his most important sermons, they begin to draw back and return to their old associations, no longer accompanying Him.

On another occasion, when Jesus went to minister in his hometown, the people in that vicinity disapproved of him and "it hindered them from acknowledging His authority," and as a result "He was not able to do even one work of power there" (Mark 6: 3, 5).

The warning given to the children of Israel just before the groundbreaking ceremony of Numbers 16 still applies to us today. If we hang around critical people, soon we find ourselves picking up their complaining ways, and lethal poison gets deposited in our hearts toward leadership. The first thing that happens is withdrawal, and then we go back to what we are familiar with—old associations—and no longer follow the true leader. Even if we don't completely abandon the one in authority, we find ourselves unable to receive from his gift any longer.

When They Criticize You

When we are on the receiving end of criticism, to say it is unpleasant is an understatement. For some, it's a blow that drives them into a pit of depression. They vow never to put themselves in a position to be criticized again. When they allow that to happen, their lives are on hold, and their gifts buried. Others learn to handle criticism by striking back with some of their own. Then, there are those who just let it roll off like they were covered with some kind of criticism-resistant substance and go on as though nothing had been said. What makes the difference?

I remember hearing a statement made by Oral Roberts—a man who, throughout his ministry, was highly criticized by both the church and the media. His thinking was, "Let the dogs bark. The train rolls on."

The late H. A. Ironside described a response to criticism this way: "If what they are saying about you is true, mend your ways. If it isn't true, forget it, and go on and serve the Lord."

I read this account about the late Kathryn Kuhlman, written by Jamie Buckingham in *Coping with Criticism*, regarding her reaction when criticized:

> For a number of years, until her death in 1976, I worked off and on with Kathryn Kuhlman as a writer. Although Miss Kuhlman was very sensitive to criticism, she never let it deter her from her goal. Instead, she used it to help her get there—always seeming to make the very best out of even the harshest criticism.
>
> Shortly after she went on nationwide television with her weekly program, she received a letter from a public school official in the little town of Iredell, Texas.
>
> "I love you and love your program," he wrote. "It would have been much better, however, if you didn't have to spend so much time tugging at your skirt trying to pull it down over your knees. It was really distracting. Why don't you wear a long dress instead?"
>
> Kathryn read the letter. "You know, he's right," she said to her secretary.
>
> She never wore another street-length dress on her TV program. A lesser person would have responded with anger, or passed it off as just another senseless remark. But she was not that sort of lesser person. She heard. She coped. She let it help her toward her goal of communicating. All of which was possible because there was no root of bitterness to give a bad taste to everything that came into her life or to anyone that presented another viewpoint.

It's wonderful to watch leaders with sound character handle criticism graciously, but the very epitome of how to do it was Jesus himself. In John 6, Jesus the Messiah delivered his pivotal sermon declaring himself the light of the world and the bread of life. He might have gotten by with that, but he insisted on adding the controversial statement about eating his flesh and drinking his blood. Criticism exploded all around his once-popular ministry like a cyclone. Before he knew it, followers who would have given their lives for him before now left in droves. A less confident minister would have chased after his supporters, defending and trying to explain what he really meant. Jesus, instead, turned to his handful of disciples who stood uncertainly by his side and asked, "Will you also go away? [And do you too desire to leave Me?]"

Peter had sense enough to declare, "Lord, to whom shall we go? You have the words (the message) of eternal life. And we have learned to believe and trust, and [more] we have come to know [surely] that You are the Holy One of God, the Christ (the Anointed One), the Son of the living God" (John 6:68–69).

Jesus did not depend on the opinions of other people. He said only what the Father told him to say and did only what God directed him to do; therefore, criticism did not shake him or move him away from his purpose or message.

Eleanor Roosevelt was reported as saying, "Nobody can make you feel inferior without your permission."

Criticism has only as much power as you give it. You can either whine because you have internalized other people's negative evaluation, or you can let it slide off your self-image like oil off a mirror and continue to grow and improve. You can't fix the holes in someone else's life with your good behavior; so if somebody criticizes you, it's their problem, not yours.

One time, the Lord spoke to me and asked, "If someone has a personality problem, whose problem is it?"

I thought for a moment and responded with this intelligent answer, "Well, it's their problem."

Then he added, "But if you respond and react to their dysfunction by taking it personally, it becomes your problem."

Live Creatively

In this fierce world with its microscope mentality that tends to examine and probe the most oblique portions of an individual's life, what can you do to salvage the integrity of relationships and keep them from deteriorating under the harsh light of criticism? The Message Bible answers that question in Galatians 6: 1–5:

> Live creatively, friends. If someone falls into sin, forgivingly restore him, saving your critical comments for yourself. You might be needing forgiveness before the day is out.
>
> Stoop down and reach out to those who are oppressed. Share their burdens, and so complete Christ's law. If you think you are too good for that, you are badly deceived.
>
> Make a careful exploration of who you are and the work you have been given, and then sink yourself into that. Don't be impressed with yourself. Don't compare yourself with others. Each of you must take responsibility for doing the creative best you can with your own life.

Be creative! Don't do what everyone else does. Forgive, restore, and use your energy to check yourself and your motives. Don't overestimate your importance or compare yourself with others. Comparison never delivers an accurate analysis. You will either think you are better than or inferior to the other person. Both attitudes will cause problems.

In the long run, it boils down to whether selfishness rules or the law of love prevails. "We who are strong [in our convictions and of robust faith] ought to bear with the failings and the frailties and the tender scruples of the weak; [we ought to help carry the doubts and qualms of others] and not to please ourselves" (Rom.15:1).

Paul gives the Romans some final words of advice on how to live free from criticism in relationships:

> Now may the God Who gives the power of patient endurance (steadfastness) and Who supplies encouragement, grant you to live in such mutual harmony and such full sympathy with one another, in accord with Christ Jesus,
>
> That together you may [unanimously] with united hearts and one voice, praise and glorify the God and Father of our Lord Jesus Christ (the Messiah). Welcome and receive [to your hearts] one another, then, even as Christ has welcomed and received you, for the glory of God. (Rom.15: 5–7)

In order to develop strong, healthy relationships, criticism has to be abolished because it always tends to tear down, destroy, and twist the perception of any association. Selfish people are critical people; critical people are always being selfish. The answer to handling criticism is to develop a robust measure of compassionate love, which receives and welcomes others just the way they are, faults and all, thus promoting growth. That's the way God accepts us. That's the way we are expected to embrace others if we want fulfilling and rewarding relationships.

"But love (affection and goodwill and benevolence) edifies and builds up and encourages one to grow [to his full stature]" (1 Cor. 8:1).

11

Dealing with Strife

I was required to memorize a poem by Eugene Field while in grade school, entitled "The Duel." It is a favorite of mine, not only because it has such a whimsical plot but because beneath the imaginary fracas that takes place between the gingham dog and the calico cat lies a glaring truth that is often dramatized in every level of relationships. The rhyme goes like this:

> The gingham dog and the calico cat
> Side by side on the table sat;
> 'Twas half-past twelve, and (what do you think!)
> Nor one nor t'other had slept a wink.
> The Old Dutch clock and the Chinese plate
> Appeared to know as sure as fate
> There was going to be a terrible spat.
> (I wasn't there; I simply state
> What was told to me by the Chinese plate!)
>
> The gingham dog went "Bow-wow-wow!"
> And the calico cat replied, "Mee-ow!"
> The air was littered, an hour or so,
> With bits of gingham and calico,
> While the Old Dutch clock in the chimney place
> Up with its hands before its face,
> For it always dreaded a family row.

(Now mind: I'm only telling you
What the Old Dutch clock declares is true.)

The Chinese plate looked very blue,
And wailed, "Oh, dear! What shall we do?"
But the gingham dog and the calico cat
Wallowed this way and tumbled that,
Employing every tooth and claw
In the awfullest way you ever saw –
And, oh! How the gingham and calico flew.
(Don't fancy I exaggerate –

I got my news from the Chinese plate.)
Next morning, where the two had sat,
They found no trace of dog or cat;
And some folks think unto this day
That burglars stole that pair away.
But the truth about the cat and pup
Is this: they ate each other up.
Now what do you really think of that?
(The Old Dutch clock it told me so,
And that is how I came to know.)

Throughout history, this type of problem occurred so many times that the apostle Paul found he needed to address it in the early church—and it's still going on today. In Galatians 5:15 he warns, "But if you bite and devour one another (in partisan strife), be careful that you (and your whole fellowship) are not consumed by one another."

In previous chapters, we discussed all the aspects of what to do and what not to do in order to build healthy relationships, but we have saved the most notorious destroyer for this chapter. Each problematic trait examined up until now was only a precursor to this big one: strife.

Strife can be like the devastation of an F5 tornado ripping a path of destruction through a relationship, leaving behind piles of raw, twisted emotions that require sometimes weeks, months, or even years to restore, if they are repaired at all. Or it can be an undercurrent, causing the very foundation of relationships to erode and eventually crumble over time. As Paul cautioned in the previous verse, strife consumes relationships.

The definition of *strife* is "angry contention, fighting, any contest for advantage or superiority, rivalry." A person who has a tendency to create strife is labeled as contentious.

That means he or she is "apt to dispute, is quarrelsome, argumentative, disagreeable, combative, and quick to produce conflict."

Right up front, we can agree that strife is about the contest for superiority in a relationship. The comment was made about a lady who seemed to fit the description of one who is contentious, "She is so determined to get her own way, she writes her diary in advance."

There is an old Jewish proverb that states, "Quarrels are the weapons of the weak." If that's true, whenever you are in a contest for superiority in a relationship, it doesn't mean you are strong, but it exposes the fact that you have an *innate weakness* in your character.

A wrong heart attitude is the breeding ground for strife. The attitude most often the culprit is *selfishness*. It tends to express itself through envy, jealousy, and covetousness. James identifies self-interest as one of the main sources of contention:

> What leads to strife (discord and feuds) and how do conflicts (quarrels and fightings) originate among

you? Do they not arise from your sensual desires that are ever warring in your bodily members?

You are jealous and covet [what others have] and your desires go unfulfilled; [so] you become murderers. [To hate is to murder as far as your hearts are concerned.] You burn with envy and anger and are not able to obtain [the gratification, the contentment, and the happiness that you seek], so you fight and war. You do not have, because you do not ask. [Or] you do ask [God for them] and yet fail to receive, because you ask with wrong purpose and evil, selfish motives. Your intention is [when you get what you desire] to spend it in sensual pleasures. (James 4:1–3)

This scripture defines the method by which strife develops in an individual. First, his desires are unfulfilled, so he becomes angry and fights for what he wants instead of seeking God. As a result, strife occurs when he expects to obtain gratification from man instead of God.

Depending on others to meet needs can be a major source of strife. God said it to me this way: "I never intended for mankind to get their self-esteem, self-image, or any of their needs met by another human being. Everything they need is in me.

"Strife comes about because you try to get your needs met from a human source. When that supply fails, offense, self-pity, and aggravation are the results. This produces strife, hurt, resentment, and bitterness, which are principal ingredients that poison relationships."

James uses the term *selfish motives* in James 4:3 as the reason God refuses to grant a request. A selfish motive is a strong, passionate desire to fulfill a lust in your own life that you are determined to bring to pass on your own, regardless of the needs or feelings of others.

Charles Kingsley, a professor and Clergyman of the Church of England in the nineteenth century, said, "If you wish to be miserable, think much about yourself, about what you want, what you like, what respect people ought to pay you, and what people think of you." So a contentious person is not only selfish but *miserable* as well.

On the other hand, a person who passes up the opportunity to get in strife is highly spoken of in Proverbs 20:3: "It is an honor for a man to cease from strife and keep aloof from it, but every fool will be quarreling."

Someone who entertains strife in his life is not only selfish and miserable, but this scripture indicates he is also a *fool*. In sharp contrast, a person who ceases from strife and stays away from it is not portrayed in the scriptures as an individual who is wimpy or weak. On the contrary, he is lauded as an honorable man.

A Man of Honor

Abraham, a man labeled the Father of Faith, knew how to trust God even in the area of strife. Genesis 13 tells us that Abraham was extremely rich in livestock and in silver and gold. Lot, his nephew, also had flocks, herds and tents, and the land was not able to nourish or support them so they could dwell together; consequently, there arose strife between their herdsmen.

Abraham said to Lot, "Let there be no strife, I beg of you, between you and me, and between your herdsmen and my herdsmen; for we are relatives" (Gen. 13:8).

To put an end to strife, Abraham told Lot he could choose any land that he desired while he, unselfishly, consented to move his vast possessions in the other direction. As a result, he alleviated strife and proved himself a man of honor.

The Lord then appeared to Abraham and gave him more land than he could have ever dreamed of possessing. The reason he received such a blessing from God was because he focused on *maintaining good relationships*, instead of fighting for his rights.

Everything Lot had was a result of his association with his uncle Abraham. By rights, Abraham was the one who should have had the first choice of the land, but he chose not to fight for his rights. Abraham, instead, *trusted* God to champion his cause, thus avoiding strife.

For Lot, his decision to choose what he perceived to be the choicest and most watered location turned out to be a disaster. Sodom and Gomorrah might have looked good on the surface, but in reality, it was a boiling pot of wickedness that brought tragedy to everyone associated with it. In the end, Lot lost everything he had worked so hard to accumulate, including his wife. The only people who survived were him and his two daughters, and that didn't turn out so well either. Because of his daughter's perverted thinking, they committed incest with their father, producing offspring that generations later became antagonists to Abraham's descendants.

Sometimes, the things we strive so hard to get or the rights we so desperately fight for become a curse instead of the blessing we think they are going to be.

Don't Tell Me I'm Wrong

There's a story about a cowboy who ambled into the local blacksmith shop and picked up a horseshoe, not realizing it had just come from the forge. He immediately dropped the hot shoe, shoved his seared hand into his pocket and tried to act nonchalant. The blacksmith half smiled and asked, "Kinda hot, wasn't it?"

"Nope," replied the cowboy, "just don't take me long to look at a horseshoe, that's all."

Just like that cowboy, most of us have difficulty admitting mistakes, and even more undeniable is our universal urge to be right. The need to be vindicated and prove that our view is correct provides the fuel kindling strife in any relationship.

Philosopher William James was once approached after a lecture on the solar system by a determined elderly lady with a theory. "We don't live on a ball rotating around the sun," she said. "We live on a crust of earth on the back of a giant turtle."

James decided to be gentle. "If your theory is correct, madam, then what does this turtle stand on?"

She replied, "The first turtle stands on the back of a second, far larger, turtle, of course."

"But what does that turtle stand on?" James asked.

The old lady crowed triumphantly, "It's no use, Mr. James—it's turtles all the way down!"

Those two accounts illustrate the stubbornness and pride that generates strife. In the book of Genesis, chapter four, we are introduced to a prime example of a person who refused to admit he was wrong. That chapter starts with the birth of Adam and Eve's first offspring, Cain and Abel. Cain became a farmer while Abel was a shepherd. No doubt they had both been instructed by their parents regarding the practice of worshiping God with a sacrifice, so we can assume they also were informed concerning the proper kind of sacrifice to offer.

Earlier, when Adam and Eve sinned, God instituted a blood sacrifice by killing a lamb and covering them with the skin, pointing to the ultimate redemption to come later that would eradicate sin through the blood of Jesus Christ.

Even though God's instructions regarding the necessity of offering a blood sacrifice is not penned down, from the account of the ensuing events, we can assume both Cain and Abel had been schooled on all the details. Instead of acquiring a lamb from Abel, Cain decided to do it his own way. He sacrificed fruit from his farm instead of what God required.

We read in verses four and five that God approved and accepted Abel's offering but rejected Cain's. As a result, Cain lost his temper and started to pout.

God confronted Cain, "Why this tantrum? Why the sulking? If you do well, won't you be accepted? And if you don't do well, sin is lying in wait for you, ready to pounce; it's out to get you, you've got to master it" (Gen. 4:6–7, MSG).

Because Cain didn't do right, and *refused* to accept responsibility for his actions, he attacked his brother and killed him. Often, that's the way it is when a person who doesn't want to change is convicted by someone who is being obedient. He will try to find something to criticize and demean in that other person. Strife will be the outcome. As for Cain, because he chose not to master the sin that was waiting to pounce on him, he chose a curse rather than a blessing.

Abraham, on the other hand, discovered that operating in the wisdom of God brought great blessings. Cain found out the hard way that bitter jealousy and contention produced all sorts of evil and vile practices—murder to be exact—and for the remainder of his life, he had to endure hardship and misery.

"For wherever there is jealousy (envy) and contention (rivalry and selfish ambition), there will also be confusion (unrest, disharmony, rebellion) and all sorts of evil and vile practices" (James 3:16).

Some people pay dearly for the right to be right and, in the end, discover they have paid far too high a price for that privilege because they wind up reaping confusion and the evil effects of strife.

Devilish Wisdom

The sin of strife is always out to get you, and it takes the wisdom of God to master it. In James 3:14–18, he discusses the two different kinds of wisdom contrasted between Abraham and Cain. The Message Bible compares these two types of wisdom:

> Mean-spirited ambition isn't wisdom. Boasting that you are wise isn't wisdom. Twisting the truth to make yourselves sound wise isn't wisdom. It's the furthest thing from wisdom—it's animal cunning, devilish conniving.
>
> Whenever you're trying to look better than others or get the better of others, things fall apart and everyone ends up at the others' throats. Real wisdom, God's wisdom, begins with a holy life and is characterized by getting along with others. It is gentle and reasonable, overflowing with mercy and blessings, not hot one day and cold the next, not two-faced.

You can develop a healthy, robust community that lives right with God and enjoy its results only if you do the hard work of getting along with each other, treating each other with dignity and honor.

Water Torture

No one really enjoys strife. Solomon, who wrote the book of Proverbs, had a lot to say about contention. His writings often refer to a contentious female, and it's no wonder; he had seven hundred wives and three hundred concubines. Can you imagine what it would be like having all those women thrown together, fighting for the attention of one man? However, these verses are not just about females; they apply to the male species as well.

Solomon evidently had some exclusive, experiential knowledge about the frustration of living around strife. On four occasions, he interrupts his flow of intellectual insight by penning down his intense dislike for dissension:

"It is better to dwell in the corner of the housetop than to share a house with a disagreeing, quarrelsome, and scolding woman" (Prov. 25:24).

"It is better to dwell in a corner of the housetop [on the flat oriental roof, exposed to all kinds of weather] than in a house shared with a nagging, quarrelsome, and faultfinding woman" (Prov. 21:9).

"The contentions of a wife are like a continual dripping [of water through a chink in the roof]" (Prov.19:13).

"A continual dripping on a day of violent showers and a contentious woman are alike" (Prov. 27:15). The Message Bible says it this way: "A nagging spouse is like the drip, drip, drip of a leaky faucet."

Have you ever tried to sleep in a house with a leaky faucet? The constant drip, drip, drip is maddening. As the night wears on, it seems to get louder and louder until your whole body rises and falls with each successive drip. It makes for a miserable night.

When I read these scriptures, especially the water-related ones, I am reminded of a method of torture I heard about. A drop of water was directed to continually fall on the head of a prisoner of war, and as a result, they would either talk or go crazy in the process.

If you are cooped up in a relationship with a contentious person, you are in your own personal torture chamber, according to Solomon. If you are in the category of being a strife-producing individual, think it not strange that others don't enjoy your company. No one enjoys being tormented. Strife brings with it a particular kind of agony.

Some of the drippings that Solomon notes are nagging, disagreeing, scolding and being quarrelsome and faultfinding, all of which are strife producing and make a person difficult to get along with.

Spirit of Strife

In James 3, the apostle indicates that the source of strife is not God. He categorizes it as demonical, meaning it comes from the devil and is propagated by demons. However, people who get in strife can't just cop out by saying, "The devil made me do it." You are the one who determines whether you get in strife or not. Every attitude that is not of God is a stronghold the devil hides behind to do his dirty work. Attitudes in your life are under your control. If you don't do something to change troublesome attitudes, the adversary will have free reign to steal, kill, and destroy the relationships in your life through dissension.

A friend of ours, a native of Nairobi, Africa, handed me a book a few years ago about a sorcerer named Mukendi. He, along with 140 others, had been transported into the spirit realm for a meeting with Satan himself. There, he was groomed to perform satanic acts. Satan had given Mukendi eight more years to live and then sent him back to earth to destabilize the church of Jesus Christ in Zaire. His orders were to destroy as many Christians as he could in the time he had left before his death.

He soon found that sanctified, born again Christians had some kind of powerful protection against his incantations, and his efforts to destroy them had no effect on their lives. He had been told by Satan that it was impossible to invade a Christian's life unless he first got them unclothed. (That's how spiritualists saw people. They were either clothed or naked. Those who were clothed were Christians and not vulnerable to his attacks, those who were naked were at his mercy.) Lucifer himself taught Mukendi how to accomplish this.

Satan told Mukendi that in the world there are three types of people: "Those you will see with clothes on have the Holy Spirit and belong to Jesus. They are our main target. It is not so easy for anyone to possess them. You have to approach them carefully. The goal is to get them completely naked spiritually."

Lucifer described the second group as those who go to church, but because they are not sanctified, they look completely naked in the spirit realm. They are vulnerable and defenseless against demonic attacks. The third category is ordinary people who are not saved. The devil regards them as his and is not worried about them.

When Mukendi was sent to labor for the devil with the intention of destabilizing the church of Jesus Christ, he worked under strictly laid out strategies, namely, to destroy Christian's love for one another. Anywhere he was successful in doing that, the church crumbled.

In the book, Mukendi disclosed that the primary way sorcerers were able to gain power over Christians was to drive them to anger. Then, their souls would be opened up, thus allowing him to introduce demons into their lives. Anyone he perceived as clothed spiritually was his target. Once he encountered such an individual, he would wait until that person spoke. Then he very often could get easy access to the unsuspecting Christian's soul through listening to what he said. Demons have no ability to access anyone who speaks carefully and remains sober. Anger and loose talk are the devil's major points of entrance.

We have a formidable adversary who is up to no good. His main purpose is to destroy every godly relationship and anyone who is serving Jesus Christ. We can't afford to be naïve when it comes to the devil's tactics. It's no wonder Paul advised believers in Ephesians 4:27–28, "When angry, do not sin; do not ever let your wrath (your exasperation, your fury or indignation) last until the sun goes down. Leave no [such] room or foothold for the devil [give no opportunity to him]."

When you slam shut the door of strife in the face of the enemy, you can succeed at keeping him and all his evil works at bay. Because strife is such a powerful tool of the devil, we know why Proverbs 6:19 reveals discord as one of the seven things that God hates. God delights in blessing his children. It must grieve his heart to see so many living under a curse as a result of strife and contention.

How to Stop Strife

In this strife-filled world, how do we escape the devastation that ravishes relationships? The only solution is simple—let go of strife. Very often, it comes down to one simple and poignant question: do you want to be right, or do you want to live in peace? Too often you can't have both. But when you decide you don't have to be right all the time, you can finally live fully and happily under the protection of the peaceful state of righteousness. Your relationships will reap marvelous benefits as a result.

Here are some practical things you can do to avoid strife if you don't want misery, guilt, and the evil and vile practices in your life that discord causes:

1. Keep the tone of your voice soft and polite. Don't whine or nag or be harsh or critical. Proverbs 15:1 declares, "A soft answer turns away wrath; but grievous words stir up anger." Proverbs 15:4 says, "A gentle tongue (with its healing power) is a tree of life, but willful contrariness in it breaks down the spirit." It has been determined that 90 percent of the friction of daily life is caused by the wrong tone of voice.

2. Keep your mouth shut. There is an old saying that states, "The best way to keep people from jumping down your throat is to keep your mouth shut." Proverbs 12:23 says it this way: "He who guards his mouth and his tongue, keeps himself from troubles." Proverbs 13:3 confirms that same principle. "He who guards his mouth keeps his life, but he who opens wide his lips will come to ruin." Finally, Proverbs

29:11 advises, "A fool utters all his anger, but a wise man keeps it back and stills it."

3. Refuse to entertain thoughts that lead to strife. A thought may seem harmless, but so is a little trickle through a hole in the dam. If allowed to continue, disaster is just around the corner. We find this principle in Proverbs 17:14. "The beginning of strife is as when water first trickles (from a crack in a dam); therefore, stop contention before it becomes worse and quarreling breaks out."

I saw a commercial on television where two inspectors walked across the face of a large dam looking for defects in the structure. Spying a little crack with water barely squirting through, the man took a wad of chewing gum from his mouth and planted it securely over the little hole. With a flourish, he declared, "That ought to fix it." Then acting as though the problem was solved, the two went on their way, never looking back, or giving the problem another thought. As soon as they turned their backs, the gum popped out, and the hole became bigger and more menacing. We, the viewer, know that because the problem had not been solved appropriately, at some point in the near future, the dam is going to burst wide open causing devastation from the tons of water that had been held back.

If you are serious about stopping strife in your life, don't underestimate the power of just a tiny, seemingly insignificant negative thought that meanders through your brain. It may appear harmless, but if allowed to continue, it can rupture the dam that is holding back bitter words and open the floodgates of contention and full-blown, vicious quarreling. It is certainly easier to stop the thoughts that come to your mind than take back words you have spoken. It is a proven fact that if you think a thought long enough, it becomes a word spoken and then ultimately a deed done. Second Corinthians 10:5 tells us to "lead every thought and purpose away captive into the obedience of Christ."

4. Sow seeds of peace. Romans 12:18–21 tells you how to do this. "If possible, as far as it depends on you, live at peace with everyone. Beloved, never avenge yourselves, but leave the way open for (God's) wrath; for it is written, Vengeance is Mine, I will repay (requite), says the Lord. But if your enemy is hungry, feed him; if he is thirsty, give him drink; for by so doing you will heap burning coals upon his head. Do not let yourself be overcome by evil, but overcome (master) evil with good."

There are two different ways to live. God offers you his wisdom, which produces peace. If you are self-cherishing, the devil can put tremendous pressure on your flesh to yield to his way of thinking, opening the door for demonic activity—and that is never good.

James 3: 17–18 describes the out-of-this-world results you get from doing it God's way:

> But the wisdom from above is first of all pure (undefiled); then it is peace-loving, courteous (considerate, gentle). [It is willing to] yield to reason, full of compassion and good fruits; it is wholehearted and straightforward, impartial and unfeigned (free from doubts, wavering, and insincerity).

And the harvest of righteousness (of conformity to God's will in thought and deed) is [the fruit of the seed] sown in peace by those who work for and make peace [in themselves and in others, that peace which means concord, agreement, and harmony between individuals, with undisturbedness, in a peaceful mind free from fears and agitating passions and moral conflicts].

The harvest of righteousness is the fruit of all of those seeds you sow when you do what you *ought to do* in a conflict instead of what you *want to do*. And the side effects aren't too bad either. Harmony in relationships and a mind undisturbed and free from agitating passions and fears are priceless.

12

Relationship Commitment

Now we get down to where the train meets the tracks. As far as it depends on you, how serious are you about transforming your life in order to live peacefully with everyone? You can't be responsible for your spouse, your children, your neighbor, or even your in-laws. You can only change yourself, and until now, everything you have learned in this book leads to this last and final decision. In order to influence every relationship for the better, can you make a commitment to alter some lifelong habits of thinking and reacting on a permanent basis?

Throughout this book, we have found the problem with most relationships is not necessarily behavior but in the attitudes of the heart. Your attitudes are the aroma of your life. An aroma can't be seen with the eye, but it will certainly determine the atmosphere of a place. You can't control someone else's attitude, but you can manage your own. Attitudes make or break a relationship.

All attitudes proceed from the *theme of your heart*. If there is a selfish theme, then the attitudes will reveal it. If you have a gracious heart filled with compassion and love for others, that too will be reflected in the climate of your relationships.

When other people evaluate you, they never just observe your outward appearance. They can detect the attitudes of your heart, which tends to draw them closer to you or causes them to withdraw. When love emanates from your heart, there will be a sweet-smelling fragrance that influences the environment when you walk into a room. Others will be attracted to you and enjoy the pleasure of your company.

The theme of your heart determines the story of your life. Pride is the ingredient that forms a hardened shield around your heart, preventing you from changing its theme. Unless pride crumbles, your heart will never change. When pride surrounds your heart, it stops up your ears, preventing you from hearing the truth. It also facilitates and amplifies the voice of the father of lies, whose whole mission is to distort truth.

You will never be able to change the theme of your heart without humility. A humble person is one who easily hears instructions from the Word of God and readily changes. That person will never have an attitude problem.

Years ago, I realized I had trouble with relationships. I was easily hurt, and self-pity was a live-in companion to me. Convinced that if other people would treat me right I could be happy, I spent considerable time and energy perfecting the art of manipulation, trying to persuade them to contribute to my well-being. It didn't work! I was miserable and depressed most of the time and had trouble allowing anyone to get close to me. After struggling for many years, God finally unwrapped a marvelous plan for me to live by. When I implemented this simple but profound blueprint, the tangled cobwebs of wrong thinking straightened out, and relationships were fun for a change. These remarkable truths changed the theme of my heart.

I call this wonderful, liberating strategy a *relationship commitment* or "the plan." It is a systematic six-point outline that will change your paradigm and transform the negatives in your personality, drastically improving your ability to get along with others. Most importantly, living according to this commitment will close the door of strife to the demons of discord, and produce peace.

As you read through this commitment, each point has a demon spirit that inhabits and is associated with the different kinds of habitual behavior. When you refuse to indulge in any of these offensive categories of conduct, it renders the devil powerless to cause dissention and strife through you.

The Plan

This book started by revealing the law that governs human relationships, which is the law of love. To unveil the plan, you must first of all submit to the law. So point number one is a fundamental decision concerning walking in love. Without this crucial choice, the rest of the plan won't work:

1. I choose to place myself under God's law of love, meeting the needs of others and looking out for their interests instead of my own, trusting that God will look after my welfare because I believe what I sow I will reap. (Phil. 2:4; Luke 6:38; Gal. 6:7) I choose to be restrained and regulated by God's commands and his will. (1 John. 3:4)

   Once you firmly resolve to make love your quest, operating from that theme in the affairs of your life, you no longer allow the *spirit of selfishness* to have free reign. Then the second point falls neatly into place:

2. I choose to live creatively, refusing to criticize others even when I think I am right and they are wrong. Instead, I will edify, build up, and encourage them out of a heart of love, affection, and goodwill and will welcome and receive them into my heart as Christ has welcomed me. (1 Cor. 8:1; Rom. 15:7)

   When you choose to strike at the heart of a *critical spirit*, refusing to give place to this weapon of division, then point number three will not be such a strong temptation:

3. I will never put demands on another individual to meet my needs. I free everyone (my spouse included) from any obligation to make me happy, content, or satisfied. Instead, I will look to God to fulfill my desires. He has promised to meet all my needs according to his riches in glory. (Phil. 4:19; Ps. 118: 5–8)

   When you take everyone off your hit list and put your complete trust in God to meet any need you might have, you have succeeded in conquering the *spirit of control* so then the next point becomes easier to carry out.

4. I refuse to be offended at anyone or by anything. In spite of how I am treated or what anyone says to me, I will quickly forgive and let it drop immediately. I will resist the temptation to entertain the offense in my thoughts, my words, or my actions.

   If you can carry out point number four successfully, the *spirit of offense* will be disarmed, and it is less likely you will have to deal with this next point so often:

5. I will never again feel sorry for myself, no matter what circumstances may come my way or how I am treated. (Phil. 4:4, 11–13)

    When you no longer have a tendency to feel sorry for yourself, then the *spirit of self-pity* can no longer bed up in your emotions or your thought life, causing oppression and depression. Then this sixth point sums up the last and final hurdle to peace and fulfillment. When it is effectively woven throughout the fabric of your life, it closes the door to the principal destroyer of relationships: a *spirit of anger.*

6. It doesn't matter what type of adverse situations I face, I will never again allow myself to become aggravated. (John 14:27)

As you read through the different sections of this relationship commitment, you encountered words like *never again*, *I refuse*, and *I choose*, indicating a vow to *always* fulfill the requirements of this pledge. The thought of never violating any of these points may be overwhelming. It may seem to be a promise impossible to keep, thus discouraging you from even trying to achieve these lofty goals. But that is just what they are. They are goals. If I wanted to be realistic, maybe I would have said, "As often as I feel like it"; or "Whenever I think I can"; or maybe, "Once in a while I will not get aggravated"; and so on.

If that were the case, then you would be right where you have been all along. If your behavior has been wrong, you have made wrong choices about how to react on a regular basis, and have experienced the consequences. If you really want to change, you can't respond as you have in the past and expect different results. It is essential to set guidelines for your behavior *ahead of time*. That's what this commitment does.

These are guidelines, and truthfully, they are impossible to achieve without the grace and power of the Holy Spirit. In order to drastically change your life, anything worth doing is impossible in the flesh, but all things are possible with God. "I have strength for all things in Christ Who empowers me [I am ready for anything and equal to anything through Him Who infuses inner strength into me; I am self-sufficient in Christ's sufficiency]" (Phil. 4:13).

The Doer of the Word Is Blessed

Jesus told us in Luke 6 about two specific houses. They were similar in many ways but with one dramatic distinction. One foundation was built on a solid rock, the other had no foundation and rested on top of a section of sand. Then the inevitable happened. A devastating storm came to both houses. The one perched on the sand was completely wiped out, destroyed, and totally ruined. But the other house had been systematically, and with considerable effort, constructed on a solid rock formation. That structure could not be shaken or even moved by the tempest. The foundation made the difference.

The point Jesus tried to get across is summed up in the question he asked in verse forty-six, "Why do you call Me, Lord, Lord, and do not [practice] what I tell you?"

In verses forty-seven and forty-eight, he revealed the secret of why that one home had the ability to withstand the hurricane strength winds and the flood that threatened to destroy it.

For everyone who comes to Me and listens to My words [in order to heed their teaching] and does them, I will show you what he is like: He is like a man building a house, who dug and went down deep and laid a foundation upon the rock; and when a flood arose, the torrent broke against that house and could not shake or move it, because it had been securely built or founded on a rock.

It is not what *you hear* that determines your stability; it's what you make the effort and take the time *to do* that counts.

One More Night with the Frogs

It's not enough to just know what the Bible says and even hear it read over and over; you have to *do what you are told to do*. Sometimes, that means crucifying your flesh and practicing something you don't feel like doing.

Over the past years, I have ministered to several young people whose lives were in a mess. I knew they were that way because of wrong choices, so I challenged them to change their way of thinking and choose a different path. On one occasion, after I had spent a couple of hours describing the blessings of walking according to God's ways as opposed to the misery and pain of living by fleshly appetites, one person informed me she was not ready to make that choice. In other words, she wasn't quite ready to give up her dysfunctional ways and live the blessed life.

That reminded me of Pharaoh when the Egyptians experienced the plagues in Moses's day. One plague was an infestation of croaking, slimy frogs. When Moses asked the king when he wanted to get deliverance from those repulsive creatures, Pharaoh said, "Tomorrow!" Why he wanted to spend one more night with the frogs, I'll never know, but that's the way a lot of people are. They have grown so familiar with the wretchedness of their lifestyle they don't want to make the effort it requires to change anything.

Where Two Ways Meet

In Matthew 7:13–14, Jesus pulls back the curtain of the natural, physical world and reveals what is a reality in the spirit realm. He shows us two ways that are available to all mankind. One is a broad way, which is unrestricted and accommodates every whim and impulse. It looks particularly inviting, and many find themselves walking on that highway; however, that road leads to death and destruction.

The other street is a narrow way and not quite as appealing. It is described in the Amplified Bible as a path that is "restricted (contracted by pressure) and straitened and compressed, but this path leads to life." It doesn't attract a large crowd because to stay on this route requires discipline and restrictions in conduct, and that's not always easy. In fact, your flesh does not like it one bit. Your selfish nature wants to be gratified, right now, and doesn't like the boundaries God's word places on it.

At any given time, you are walking on one of the two roads, headed for its respective destination. It's much like the challenge Moses offered the children of Israel in Deuteronomy 30:19. He had just finished describing the blessings that would overtake them if they listened to and obeyed God, but he also strongly warned them about the curses that would come upon them if they did not observe God's commandments or listen to his voice. In chapter thirty, he presented them with a choice: blessing or cursing, life or death. Finally, with all the persuasion he could muster, Moses announced in a loud, commanding voice, "Choose life!"

That's what I have done through the pages of this book. I have shown you two ways. The broad way paved with selfishness allows you to do what you feel like doing, when you feel like it, in your own way, and then I have taken you on a tour down the narrow way that is regulated and restrained by God's commandment of love. Step by step, you have been shown how to move from a selfish life filled with frustration and turmoil in relationships onto a glorious, peaceful highway of love, free from the destruction and harm unbridled in the world we live in. To take advantage of the possibilities God holds out, you must make a choice. This is how the Lord spoke to me about this choice:

> If my word is your guideline for living, and my voice you instantly obey.
> Your feet will be firmly established, on the straight and narrow way.
> Then devastation can be all around you, but only with your eyes will you see;
> The destruction that comes to the disobedient, but harm will not come nigh thee.
> Then you can stand with confident assurance, in victory the whole world can see,
> And tell them with great conviction: it pays to live scripturally!

So I present to you two ways. Blessing or cursing. Life or death. My sincere prayer for you is, choose life!

13

Relationship Commitment
The Plan

In order to have peace in my life and in every relationship, I make a quality decision with the help of the grace of God to commit to the following:

1. I choose to put myself under God's law of love, meeting the needs of others while looking out for their interests instead of my own, trusting that God will look after my welfare because I believe what I sow I will reap. (Phil. 2:4; Luke 6:38; Gal. 6:7) I choose to allow God's commands and his will to regulate and restrain my life. (1 John. 3:4)

2. I choose to live creatively, refusing to criticize others even when I think I am right and they are wrong. Instead, I will edify, build up, and encourage them out of a heart of love, affection, and goodwill, and will welcome and receive them into my heart as Christ has welcomed me (1 Cor. 8:1; Rom. 15:7).

3. I will never put demands on another individual to meet my needs. I free everyone, my spouse included, from any obligation to make me happy, content, or satisfied. Instead, I will look to God to fulfill my desires. He has promised to meet all of my needs

according to his riches in glory (Phil. 4:19; Ps. 118: 5–8).

4. I refuse to be offended at anyone or by anything. In spite of how I am treated or what anyone says to me, I will quickly forgive and let it drop immediately. I will resist the temptation to entertain the offense in my thoughts, my words, or my actions.

5. I will never again feel sorry for myself, no matter what circumstances may come my way or how I am treated (Phil. 4:4, 11–13).

6. It doesn't matter what type of adverse situations I am faced with; I will never again allow myself to become aggravated (John 14:27).

Signed: _____

Date: _____

Witnessed and notarized by the Holy Spirit.

Bibliography

Buckingham, Jamie. 1978. *Coping with Criticism.* Plainfield, New Jersey: Logos International.

Chapman, Gary. 2004. *The Five Love Languages.* Chicago: Northfield Publishing.

Draper, Edythe. 1992. *Draper's Quotations for the Christian World.* Wheaten, IL: Tyndale House Publishers, Inc. STEP Files Copyright © 2005. QuickVerse.

Field, Eugene. 1971. "The Duel." *Childcraft: The How and Why Library.* Chicago: Field Enterprises

Flanigan, Beverly. 2005. "Forgiving the Unforgivable: Overcoming the Bitter Legacy of Intimate Wounds." *Curves.* December 2005.

Kaniaki, D.D., and Mukendi. 1991. *Snatched from Satan's Claws.* Nairobi, Kenya: Enkei Media Services Ltd.

Leaf, Caroline. 2009. *Who Switched off My Brain?: Controlling Toxic Thoughts and Emotions.* Place of Publication Not Identified: Inprov.

Matousek, Mark. "Quit your Pain." *AARP Magazine.* May/June 2006

Meyer, Joyce. 2003. *Beauty for Ashes.* New York: Warner Faith.

Michaud, Ellen. "Forgiving the Unforgivable: Diane" *Curves.* December 2005.

Phillips, Bob. 1993. *Phillips' Book of Great Thoughts and Funny Sayings: A Stupendous Collection of Quotes, Quips, Epigrams, Witticisms, and Humorous Comments: For Personal Enjoyment and Ready Reference.* Wheaton, IL: Tyndale House Publishers, Inc. STEP Files Copyright © 2005. QuickVerse.

Compiled for Quick Verse by Ruth Peters 1995. *Illustrations of Bible Truths.* Chattanooga, TN: AMG International, Inc. STEP Files Copyright © 2005. QuickVerse.

Tenney, Tommy. 2004. *Hadassah: One Night with the King.* Bloomington, Minnesota: Bethany House Publishers.

The Medical Institute for Sexual Health. Austin. https// www.medinstiture.org

The Painter's Keys Resource of Art Quotations. http// painterskeys.com

http://www.google.com/intl/en/privacypolicy.html.]

Also By Margaret Mendenhall

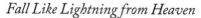

Fall Like Lightning from Heaven

John's world is filled with turmoil as the bubonic plague ravages his congregation. Can these hideous deaths be God's will? If God is good, then why are bad things happening to good people? As John desperately searches through the sacred text, he discovers the epic battle between light and darkness. His quest uncovers secrets that could cause the defeat of the wicked spirit who fell like lightning from heaven. Margaret Mendenhall takes you behind the scenes in an inspirational and eye-opening journey that exposes the lies and implications that endeavor to defame the character of God. Can the battle for mankind's freedom be won—or is the price too high?

To purchase a copy, order from yorkshirepublishing. com, amazon.com, mendenhallministries.com or where books are sold.

Dawn of the Silver Moon

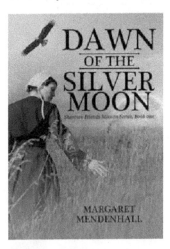

Revenge plunges Lucy Hiatt, who has grown up in the Quaker lifestyle, into the strange world of the Shawnee Indians where she discovers simple faith in God's word can build a bridge between two cultures. Taken captive by a group of Shawnee and forced to travel from Kansas Territory to Indian Territory, Lucy struggles across a raging river at flood stage, faces a killer tornado, and endures threats from Black Crow who wants to kill and scalp her or make her his woman to satisfy his vengeance. In the end, she must choose between a routine life with Jacob or opportunities among the Shawnee with Soaring Eagle. With Black Crow's threats looming, will she live long enough to make that choice?

To purchase a copy, order from yorkshirepublishing. com, amazon.com, mendenhallministries.com or where books are sold.

Contact Information

For speaking engagements or comments, contact:

Margaret Mendenhall
Victory Center Church P.O. Box 128
Guymon, OK 73942
e-mail: pastorm@victorycenter.org
www.mendenhallministries.com
Phone: 580-338-5616

CPSIA information can be obtained
at www.ICGtesting.com
Printed in the USA
FFHW010204111019
55479195-61278FF